2018 SQA Past Papers with Answers

Advanced Higher
BIOLOGY

2016, 2017 & 2018 Exams

Hodder Gibson Study Skills Advice – Advanced Higher Biology	– page 3
Hodder Gibson Study Skills Advice – General	– page 5
2016 EXAM	– page 7
2017 EXAM	– page 53
2018 EXAM	– page 101
ANSWERS	– page 149

HODDER GIBSON
AN HACHETTE UK COMPANY

This book contains the official 2016, 2017 and 2018 Exams for Advanced Higher Biology, with associated SQA-approved answers modified from the official marking instructions that accompany the paper.

In addition the book contains study skills advice. This advice has been specially commissioned by Hodder Gibson, and has been written by experienced senior teachers and examiners in line with the Advanced Higher syllabus and assessment outlines. This is not SQA material but has been devised to provide further guidance for Advanced Higher examinations.

Hodder Gibson is grateful to the copyright holders, as credited on the final page of the Answer section, for permission to use their material. Every effort has been made to trace the copyright holders and to obtain their permission for the use of copyright material. Hodder Gibson will be happy to receive information allowing us to rectify any error or omission in future editions.

Hachette UK's policy is to use papers that are natural, renewable and recyclable products and made from wood grown in sustainable forests. The logging and manufacturing processes are expected to conform to the environmental regulations of the country of origin.

Orders: please contact Bookpoint Ltd, 130 Park Drive, Milton Park, Abingdon, Oxon OX14 4SE. Telephone: (44) 01235 827827. Fax: (44) 01235 400454. Lines are open 9.00–5.00, Monday to Saturday, with a 24-hour message answering service. Visit our website at www.hoddereducation.co.uk. Hodder Gibson can also be contacted directly at hoddergibson@hodder.co.uk

This collection first published in 2018 by
Hodder Gibson, an imprint of Hodder Education,
An Hachette UK Company
211 St Vincent Street
Glasgow G2 5QY

Advanced Higher 2016, 2017 and 2018 Exam Papers and Answers © Scottish Qualifications Authority. Study Skills section © Hodder Gibson. All rights reserved. Apart from any use permitted under UK copyright law, no part of this publication may be reproduced or transmitted in any form or by any means, electronic or mechanical, including photocopying and recording, or held within any information storage and retrieval system, without permission in writing from the publisher or under licence from the Copyright Licensing Agency Limited. Further details of such licences (for reprographic reproduction) may be obtained from the Copyright Licensing Agency Limited, www.cla.co.uk.

Typeset by Aptara, Inc.

Printed in the UK

A catalogue record for this title is available from the British Library

ISBN: 978-1-5104-5594-8

2 1

2019 2018

Introduction

Advanced Higher Biology

The practice papers in this book give an overall and comprehensive coverage of assessment of **Knowledge** and skills of **Scientific Inquiry** for Advanced Higher Biology.

We recommend that you download and print a copy of the Advanced Higher Biology Course Assessment Specification (CAS) pages 8–17 from the SQA website at www.sqa.org.uk.

The Course

The Advanced Higher Biology Course consists of three National Units. These are Cells and Proteins, Organisms and Evolution, and Investigative Biology. In each of the Units you will be assessed on your ability to demonstrate and apply knowledge of Biology and to demonstrate and apply skills of scientific inquiry.

You must also complete a project, the purpose of which is to allow you to carry out an in-depth investigation of a Biology topic and produce a project–report. You will also take a Course examination.

How the Course is graded

To achieve a Course award for Advanced Higher Biology you must pass all three National Unit Assessments which will be assessed by your school or college on a pass or fail basis. The grade you get depends on the following two Course assessments, which are set and graded by SQA.

1. The project is worth 25% of the grade and is marked out of 30 marks. The majority of the marks will be awarded for applying scientific inquiry skills. The other marks will be awarded for applying related knowledge and understanding.
2. A written Course examination is worth the remaining 75% of the grade. The examination is marked out of 90 marks, 60–70 of which are for the demonstration and application of knowledge with the balance for skills of scientific inquiry.

This book should help you practise the examination part! To pass Advanced Higher Biology with a C grade you will need about 50% of the 120 marks available for the project and the Course examination combined. For a B you will need roughly 60% and, for an A, roughly 70% of the marks available.

The Course examination

The Course examination is a single question paper divided into two sections.

- The first section is an objective test with 25 multiple choice items worth 25 marks.
- The second section is a mix of restricted and extended response questions worth between 1 and 9 marks each for a total of 65 marks. The majority of the marks test knowledge, with an emphasis on the application of knowledge. The remainder test the application of scientific inquiry, analysis and problem solving skills. The first question is usually an extensive data question and there are two extended response questions, one for about 4–5 marks and the other for about 8–10 marks – the longer extended response question will normally have a choice and is usually the last question in the paper.

Altogether, there are 90 marks and you will have 2 hours and 30 minutes to complete the paper. The majority of the marks will be straightforward and linked to grade C but some questions are more demanding and are linked to grade A.

General hints and tips

You should have a copy of the Course Assessment Specification (CAS) for Advanced Higher Biology (you can download it from the SQA website). It is worth spending some time looking at this document, as it indicates what you can be tested on in your examination.

This book contains three practice Advanced Higher Biology examination papers. All three are past exam papers. Each paper can be attempted in its entirety, or groups of questions on a particular topic or skill area can be attempted. If you are trying a whole examination paper from this book, give yourself a maximum of 2 hours and 30 minutes to complete it. The questions in each paper are laid out roughly in Unit order. Make sure that you spend time in using the answer section to mark your own work – it is especially useful if you can get someone to help you with this.

The marking instructions give acceptable answers with alternatives. You could even grade your work on an A–D basis. The following hints and tips are related to examination techniques as well as avoiding common mistakes. Remember that if you hit problems with a question, you should ask your teacher for help.

Section 1

25 multiple-choice items **25 marks**

- Answer on a grid.
- Do not spend more than 30 minutes on this section.
- Some individual questions might take longer to answer than others – this is quite normal and make sure you use scrap paper if a calculation or any working is needed.
- Some questions can be answered instantly – again, this is normal.
- Do not leave blanks – complete the grid for each question as you work through.
- Try to answer each question in your head without looking at the options. If your answer is there you are home and dry!
- If you are not certain, it is sometimes best to choose the answer that seemed most attractive on first reading the answer options.
- If you are guessing, try to eliminate options before making your guess. If you can eliminate three, you will be left with the correct answer even if you do not recognise it!

Section 2

Restricted and extended response **65 marks**

- Spend about 2 hours on this section.
- A clue to your answer length is the mark allocation – questions restricted to 1 mark can be quite short. If there are 2–3 marks available, your answer will need to be extended and may well have two, three or even four parts.
- The questions are usually laid out in Unit sequence but remember that some questions are designed to cover more than one Unit.
- The C-type questions usually start with "State", "Identify", "Give" or "Name" and often need only a single sentence in response. They will usually be for 1 mark each.
- Questions that begin with "Explain", "Suggest" and "Describe" are usually A-type questions and are likely to have more than one part to the full answer. You will usually have to write a sentence or two and there may be 2 or even 3 marks available.
- Make sure you read over the question twice **before** trying to answer – there will be very important information within the question and underlining or highlighting key words is good technique.
- Using abbreviations like DNA and ATP is fine. The Advanced Higher Biology Course Assessment Specification (CAS) will give you the acceptable abbreviations.

- Don't worry if the questions are in unfamiliar contexts, that's the idea! Just keep calm and read the questions carefully.
- In the large data question (Q1), it is good technique to read the whole stem and then skim the data groups before starting to answer any of the parts.
- In the large data question (Q1), be aware that the first piece of data presented should give the main theme of the question.
- In experimental questions, you must be aware of the different classes of variables, why controls are needed and how reliability and validity might be improved. It is worth spending time on these ideas – they are essential and will come up year after year.
- Note that information which is additional to the main stem may be given within a question part – if it's there, you will need it!
- If instructions in the question ask you to refer to specific groups of data, follow these and don't go beyond them.
- Remember that a conclusion can be seen from data, whereas an explanation will usually require you to supply some background knowledge as well.
- Note that in your answer, you may be asked to "use data to…" – it is essential that you do this.
- Remember to "use values from the graph" when describing graphical information in words, if you are asked to do so.
- Look out for graphs with two Y-axes – these need extra special concentration and anyone can make a mistake!
- In numerical answers, it's good technique to show working and supply units.
- Answers to calculations will not usually have more than two decimal places.
- You should round any numerical answers as appropriate, but two decimal places should be acceptable.
- Ensure that you take error bars into account when evaluating the effects of treatments.
- Do not leave blanks. Always have a go, using the language in the question if you can.

Good luck!

Remember that the rewards for passing Advanced Higher Biology are well worth it! Your pass will help you get the future you want for yourself. In the exam, be confident in your own ability. If you're not sure how to answer a question, trust your instincts and just give it a go anyway. Keep calm and don't panic! GOOD LUCK!

Study Skills – what you need to know to pass exams!

General exam revision: 20 top tips

When preparing for exams, it is easy to feel unsure of where to start or how to revise. This guide to general exam revision provides a good starting place, and, as these are very general tips, they can be applied to all your exams.

1. Start revising in good time.

Don't leave revision until the last minute – this will make you panic and it will be difficult to learn. Make a revision timetable that counts down the weeks to go.

2. Work to a study plan.

Set up sessions of work spread through the weeks ahead. Make sure each session has a focus and a clear purpose. What will you study, when and why? Be realistic about what you can achieve in each session, and don't be afraid to adjust your plans as needed.

3. Make sure you know exactly when your exams are.

Get your exam dates from the SQA website and use the timetable builder tool to create your own exam schedule. You will also get a personalised timetable from your school, but this might not be until close to the exam period.

4. Make sure that you know the topics that make up each course.

Studying is easier if material is in manageable chunks – why not use the SQA topic headings or create your own from your class notes? Ask your teacher for help on this if you are not sure.

5. Break the chunks up into even smaller bits.

The small chunks should be easier to cope with. Remember that they fit together to make larger ideas. Even the process of chunking down will help!

6. Ask yourself these key questions for each course:

- Are all topics compulsory or are there choices?
- Which topics seem to come up time and time again?
- Which topics are your strongest and which are your weakest?

Use your answers to these questions to work out how much time you will need to spend revising each topic.

7. Make sure you know what to expect in the exam.

The subject-specific introduction to this book will help with this. Make sure you can answer these questions:

- How is the paper structured?
- How much time is there for each part of the exam?
- What types of question are involved? These will vary depending on the subject so read the subject-specific section carefully.

8. Past papers are a vital revision tool!

Use past papers to support your revision wherever possible. This book contains the answers and mark schemes too – refer to these carefully when checking your work. Using the mark scheme is useful; even if you don't manage to get all the marks available first time when you first practise, it helps you identify how to extend and develop your answers to get more marks next time – and of course, in the real exam.

9. Use study methods that work well for you.

People study and learn in different ways. Reading and looking at diagrams suits some students. Others prefer to listen and hear material – what about reading out loud or getting a friend or family member to do this for you? You could also record and play back material.

10. There are three tried and tested ways to make material stick in your long-term memory:

- Practising – e.g. rehearsal, repeating
- Organising – e.g. making drawings, lists, diagrams, tables, memory aids
- Elaborating – e.g. incorporating the material into a story or an imagined journey

11. Learn actively.

Most people prefer to learn actively – for example, making notes, highlighting, redrawing and redrafting, making up memory aids, or writing past paper answers. A good way to stay engaged and inspired is to mix and match these methods – find the combination that best suits you. This is likely to vary depending on the topic or subject.

12. Be an expert.

Be sure to have a few areas in which you feel you are an expert. This often works because at least some of them will come up, which can boost confidence.

13. Try some visual methods.

Use symbols, diagrams, charts, flashcards, post-it notes etc. Don't forget – the brain takes in chunked images more easily than loads of text.

14. Remember – practice makes perfect.

Work on difficult areas again and again. Look and read – then test yourself. You cannot do this too much.

15. Try past papers against the clock.

Practise writing answers in a set time. This is a good habit from the start but is especially important when you get closer to exam time.

16. Collaborate with friends.

Test each other and talk about the material – this can really help. Two brains are better than one! It is amazing how talking about a problem can help you solve it.

17. Know your weaknesses.

Ask your teacher for help to identify what you don't know. Try to do this as early as possible. If you are having trouble, it is probably with a difficult topic, so your teacher will already be aware of this – most students will find it tough.

18. Have your materials organised and ready.

Know what is needed for each exam:
- Do you need a calculator or a ruler?
- Should you have pencils as well as pens?
- Will you need water or paper tissues?

19. Make full use of school resources.

Find out what support is on offer:
- Are there study classes available?
- When is the library open?
- When is the best time to ask for extra help?
- Can you borrow textbooks, study guides, past papers, etc.?
- Is school open for Easter revision?

20. Keep fit and healthy!

Try to stick to a routine as much as possible, including with sleep. If you are tired, sluggish or dehydrated, it is difficult to see how concentration is even possible. Combine study with relaxation, drink plenty of water, eat sensibly, and get fresh air and exercise – all these things will help more than you could imagine. Good luck!

ADVANCED HIGHER

2016

National Qualifications 2016

X707/77/02

**Biology
Section 1 — Questions**

MONDAY, 9 MAY
9:00 AM – 11:30 AM

Instructions for the completion of Section 1 are given on *Page two* of your question and answer booklet X707/77/01.

Record your answers on the answer grid on *Page three* of your question and answer booklet.

Before leaving the examination room you must give your question and answer booklet to the Invigilator; if you do not, you may lose all the marks for this paper.

SECTION 1 — 25 marks
Attempt ALL questions

1. An experiment was set up to measure the activity of an enzyme using a substrate that produced a coloured product. The absorbance of the coloured product was measured using a colorimeter.

   Which row in the table describes the variable being measured?

	discrete	continuous	qualitative	quantitative
A	✓		✓	
B	✓			✓
C		✓	✓	
D		✓		✓

2. The diagram below shows the cell types used in the production of monoclonal antibodies.

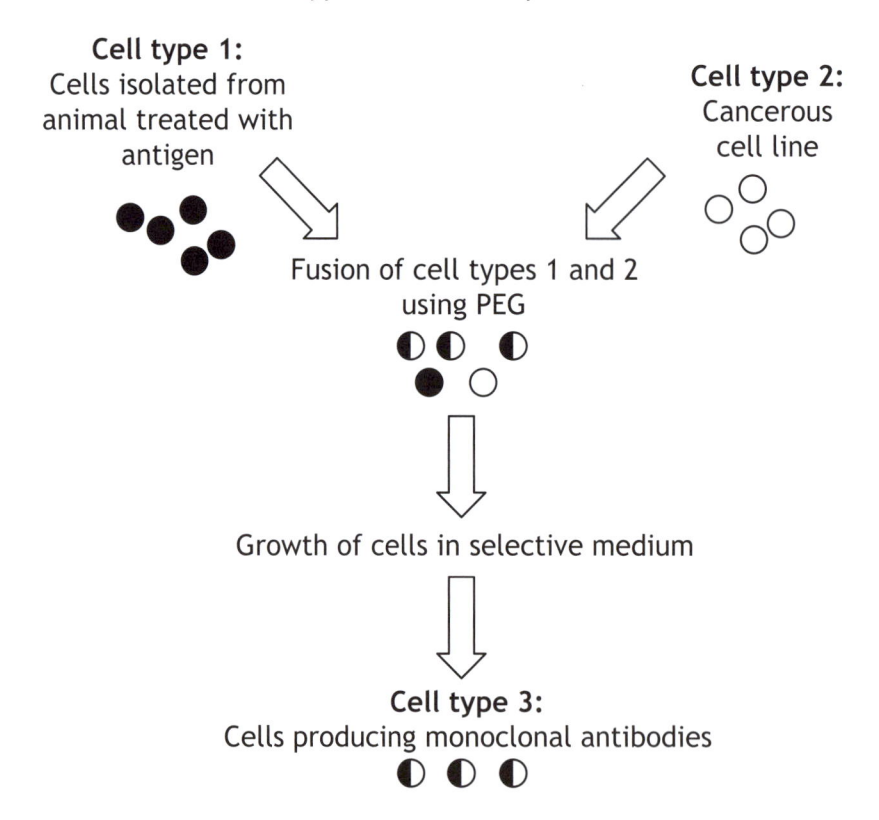

   Cell type 1: Cells isolated from animal treated with antigen

   Cell type 2: Cancerous cell line

   Fusion of cell types 1 and 2 using PEG

   Growth of cells in selective medium

   Cell type 3: Cells producing monoclonal antibodies

   Which row in the table identifies cell types 1, 2 and 3?

	Cell type 1	Cell type 2	Cell type 3
A	B lymphocyte	myeloma	hybridoma
B	myeloma	hybridoma	B lymphocyte
C	hybridoma	myeloma	B lymphocyte
D	myeloma	B lymphocyte	hybridoma

3. The diagram below represents a transmembrane protein. Some of the amino acids in the protein have been identified.

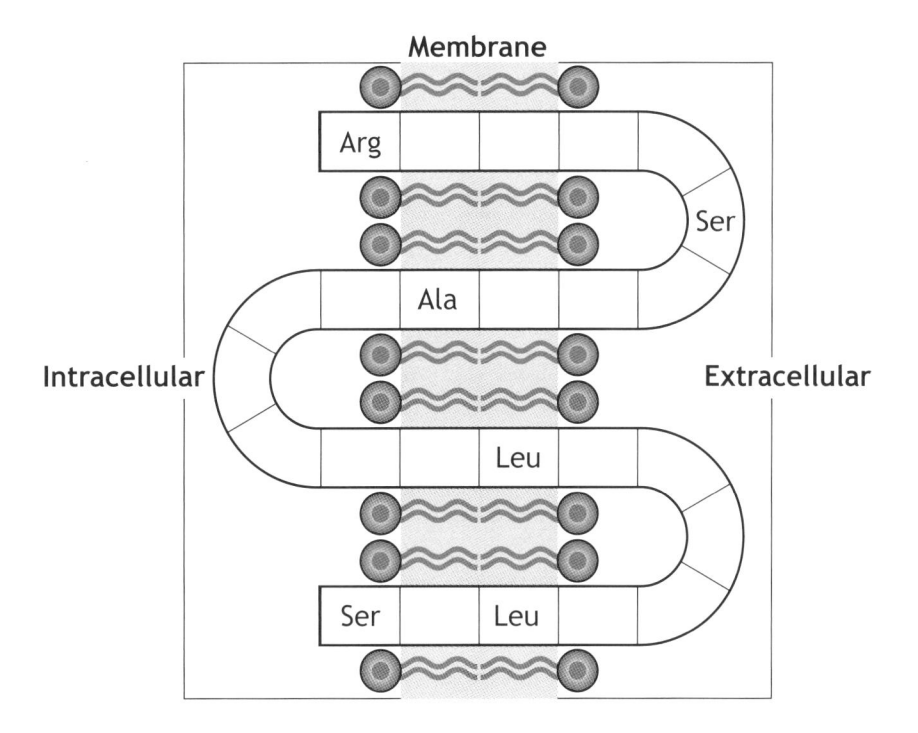

Which row in the table classifies the amino acids shown in this protein?

	Arginine (Arg)	Alanine (Ala)	Leucine (Leu)	Serine (Ser)
A	polar	hydrophobic	hydrophobic	polar
B	hydrophobic	polar	hydrophobic	polar
C	polar	hydrophobic	polar	hydrophobic
D	hydrophobic	polar	polar	hydrophobic

[Turn over

Questions 4 and 5 refer to the following information.

During muscle contraction, the protein myosin moves along an actin protein filament by the head of the myosin detaching from the actin, swinging forward and rebinding, as shown in the diagram.

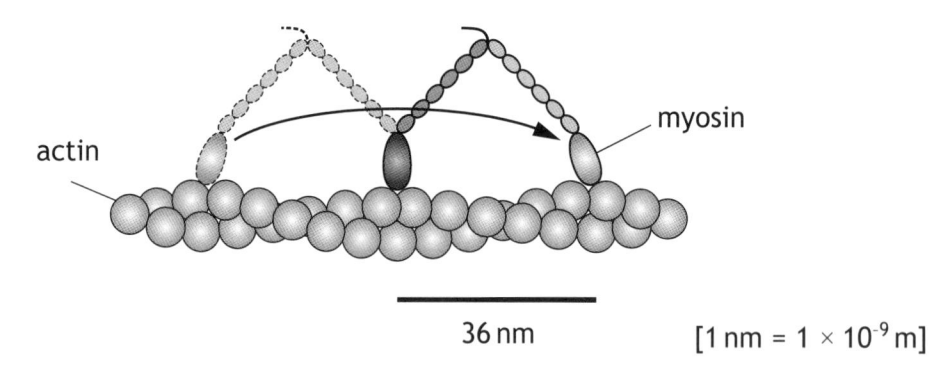

36 nm   [1 nm = 1×10^{-9} m]

4. This reversible conformational change can be brought about by binding of ATP to the myosin head followed by hydrolysis and release of phosphate and ADP.

   The myosin head is acting as

   A   a kinase

   B   an ATPase

   C   a proteinase

   D   a phosphatase.

5. When the myosin head detaches and swings forward it moves a distance of 36 nanometres (nm).

   Myosin has been observed to move at a speed of 18×10^3 nm s^{-1}.

   How many times will the myosin head detach and swing forward in one second?

   A   50

   B   200

   C   500

   D   2000

6. In animal rod cells rhodopsin absorbs a photon of light initiating the following cell events.

   1   nerve impulse is generated
   2   sufficient product formation is triggered
   3   activation of hundreds of G-protein molecules
   4   activation of hundreds of molecules of an enzyme

   The correct order of events is

   A   4, 2, 1, 3

   B   3, 4, 2, 1

   C   4, 3, 1, 2

   D   3, 2, 4, 1.

7. In multicellular organisms, only target cells respond to a specific signal because

   A   signalling molecules only come into contact with target cells
   B   only target cells have receptor molecules for the signalling molecule
   C   non-target cells do not respond when the signalling molecule binds to its receptor
   D   receptor molecules in non-target cells do not change conformation when the signalling molecule binds.

8. The hormone thyroxine is

   A   hydrophobic and unable to pass through the cell membrane
   B   hydrophilic and unable to pass through the cell membrane
   C   hydrophobic and able to pass through the cell membrane
   D   hydrophilic and able to pass through the cell membrane.

9. Biological molecules move over short distances by diffusion. The time taken for diffusion can be calculated using the equation below.

   $$t = \frac{x^2}{2D}$$

   t = time taken (seconds)
   x = distance travelled by the diffusing molecule (cm)
   D = diffusion co-efficient (cm^2 per second)

   Acetylcholine is a neurotransmitter with a diffusion co-efficient of 4×10^{-6} cm^2 per second. The gap across the synapse is 5×10^{-6} cm wide.

   How many seconds would it take acetylcholine to cross the synapse?

   A   1·250
   B   6·250 × 10^{-6}
   C   3·125 × 10^{-6}
   D   1·600 × 10^{-6}

10. Type 1 diabetes is caused by

   A   excessive production of insulin
   B   loss of insulin receptor function
   C   failure of GLUT4 to respond to insulin binding
   D   insufficient production of insulin.

[Turn over

11. An enzyme-controlled reaction is taking place in optimum conditions in the presence of a large surplus of substrate.

    Conditions can be altered by

    1 increasing the temperature
    2 adding a positive modulator
    3 increasing enzyme concentration
    4 increasing substrate concentration.

    Product yield would be increased by

    A 1 and 2
    B 2 and 3
    C 2 and 4
    D 3 and 4.

12. At which phase of the cell cycle is the retinoblastoma protein phosphorylated allowing progression to the next phase of the cycle?

    A G1
    B S
    C G2
    D M

13. The diagram below shows possible outcomes for a cell following DNA damage. Protein X is involved in all three outcomes.

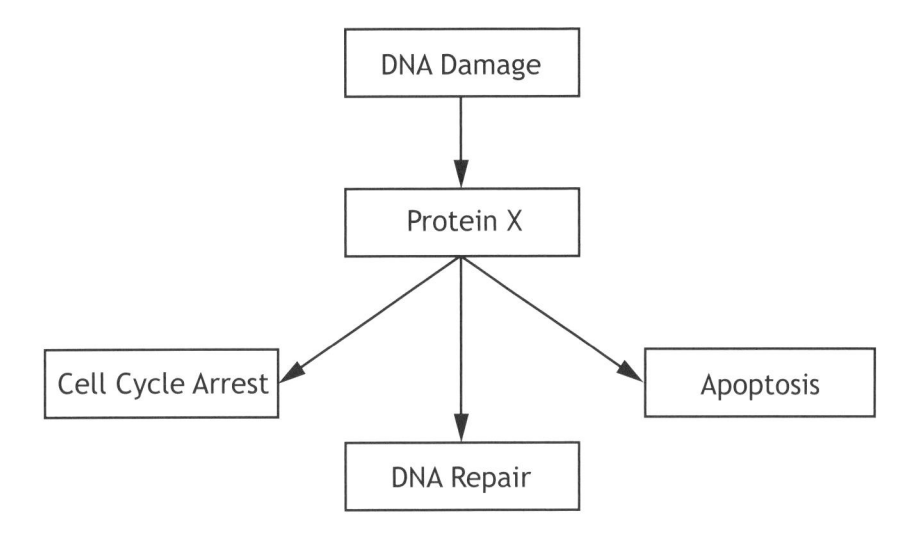

```
           DNA Damage
               ↓
           Protein X
          ↙    ↓    ↘
Cell Cycle Arrest  DNA Repair   Apoptosis
```

Protein X is

A Rb

B p53

C Cdk

D caspase.

14. Two reagents used in testing for the presence of carbohydrates are iodine solution, which turns blue-black in the presence of starch, and Benedict's solution, which turns brick red in the presence of maltose.

In an investigation of the breakdown of starch into maltose by the enzyme amylase, which of the following would be a positive control?

A Maltose alone turns Benedict's solution brick red.

B Starch treated with amylase turns Benedict's solution brick red.

C Starch alone tested with Benedict's solution remains blue.

D Starch treated with amylase does not change the colour of iodine solution.

[Turn over

15. The diagram below shows some phyla in the animal kingdom.

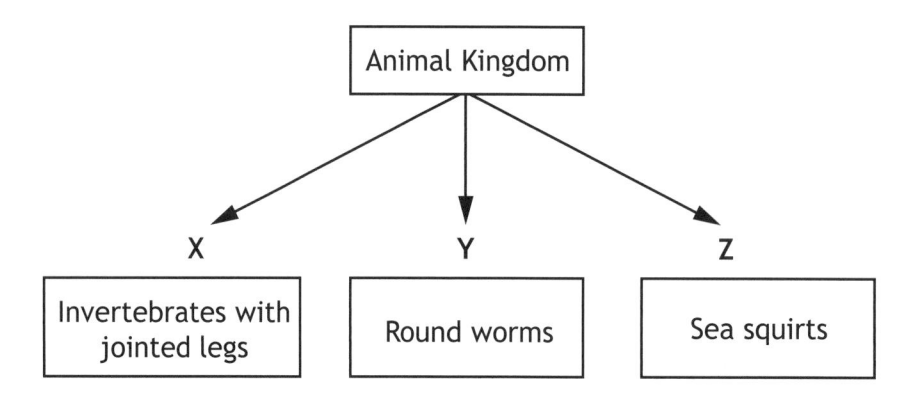

```
                    Animal Kingdom
                   /      |      \
                  X       Y       Z
     Invertebrates with  Round worms   Sea squirts
       jointed legs
```

Which row in the table identifies the phyla X, Y and Z?

	Phylum		
	X	Y	Z
A	Chordata	Nematoda	Arthropoda
B	Arthropoda	Nematoda	Chordata
C	Nematoda	Arthropoda	Chordata
D	Arthropoda	Chordata	Nematoda

16. Which of the following descriptions of animal behaviour avoids the use of anthropomorphism?

A In some primate species, alpha males often bully lower-ranking animals.

B In late summer, worker bees like to visit heather flowers.

C The grin on the chimpanzee's face showed that it was amused by the gesture.

D The male moth is attracted to the female by the scent molecules that she emits.

17. A population of chafer beetles were damaging the tees and greens of a golf course. Results from a mark and recapture study suggested a population size that was too small to account for the extent of the damage caused.

One possible reason for this is that the

A white paint used to mark the beetles washed off some of them before the recapture

B white paint used to mark the beetles made them more visible to predators than unmarked beetles

C total number of beetles in the recaptured sample was less than the number first captured and marked

D marked beetles did not have enough time, after release, to spread out and mix with the rest of the population.

18. Ellis-van Creveld syndrome is a rare genetic condition. It is much more common in an isolated population in North America, which was founded by a small number of individuals, than in the general population.

The most likely explanation for this is

A natural selection

B sexual selection

C random mutation

D genetic drift.

19. The frequency of a given allele in a population is a measure of how common that allele is as a proportion of the total number of copies of all alleles at a specific locus. For a locus with one dominant allele (A) and one recessive allele (a), the frequency of the dominant allele (p) and the frequency of the recessive allele (q) can be used to calculate the genetic variation of a population using the equations below.

$p + q = 1$ p = frequency of A allele
q = frequency of a allele

$p^2 + 2pq + q^2 = 1$ p^2 = frequency of homozygous (AA) individuals
q^2 = frequency of homozygous (aa) individuals
$2pq$ = frequency of heterozygous (Aa) individuals

If the allele frequency of the recessive allele is 0·7, the proportion of individuals that would be heterozygous is

A 0·09

B 0·21

C 0·42

D 0·49.

[Turn over

20. In the fruit fly *Drosophila melanogaster* the gene for eye colour is sex-linked. The allele for red eye (R) is dominant to the allele for white eye (r).

A cross between two flies produced the offspring shown in the table below.

Sex of offspring	Number with white eyes	Number with red eyes
female	23	22
male	21	22

The genotypes of the parents in this cross were

A X^rX^r and X^RY

B X^RX^r and X^rY

C X^RX^r and X^RY

D X^RX^R and X^rY.

21. Which row in the table best describes r-selected species?

	Number of offspring	Offspring survival rate	Parental care
A	many	low	little
B	few	high	extensive
C	many	high	extensive
D	few	low	little

22. Shags and cormorants both belong to the genus *Phalacrocorax*. They look very similar and nest near each other on the same cliffs. The table below shows the main components of each bird's diet.

Prey	Percentage composition of diet	
	Shag (Phalacrocorax aristotelis)	Cormorant (Phalacrocorax carbo)
sand eels	33	0
sprats	49	1
flatfish	1	26
shrimps	2	33
gobies	4	17
other fish	4	18

The data in the table show

A competitive exclusion

B competition within each species

C resource partitioning

D the fundamental niche of each species.

[Turn over

23. A species of parasitic wasp (*Nasonia vitripennis*) lays its eggs in the larvae of flies where the eggs develop. This species displays a behaviour called *"superparasitism"* where, following the laying of eggs by one wasp, a second wasp may superparasitise the same host by also laying its eggs.

Researchers investigated the effects of superparasitism on the brood size and sex ratio of offspring in this species. Results were compared to a control that had been parasitised only once. Researchers were able to distinguish between the offspring of the first and second wasp.

Results are shown in the table below.

Offspring	Degree of parasitism		Single parasitism control
	Superparasitism		
	Wasp 1	Wasp 2	
brood size	18 ± 3	17 ± 4	20 ± 2
percentage of males	7 ± 2	22 ± 4	6 ± 1

The following statements refer to the data in the table.

1. Superparasitism significantly increased the percentage of males produced by both wasp 1 and wasp 2.
2. Superparasitism significantly increased the percentage of males produced by wasp 2 only.
3. Superparasitism had no significant effect on brood size.
4. Superparasitism significantly decreased the brood size produced by wasps 1 and 2.

Which of these statements are valid conclusions supported by the data?

A   1 and 3
B   1 and 4
C   2 and 3
D   2 and 4

24. The statements below describe events that occur following the engulfing of a pathogen by a phagocyte of the mammalian immune system.

    P   long term survival of lymphocytes
    Q   antigen presentation to lymphocytes
    R   antibody production by lymphocytes
    S   clonal selection of B lymphocytes

    The correct sequence in which these events occur is

    A   Q, R, S, P
    B   R, Q, P, S
    C   S, Q, P, R
    D   Q, S, R, P.

25. Florida scrubjays have evolved a co-operative breeding system in which helper birds assist breeding pairs in raising young. The table below compares the effect of helpers on the breeding success of birds that are either experienced or inexperienced breeders.

Breeding experience of breeding pairs	Average number of offspring reared	
	Without helpers	With helpers
inexperienced	1·24	2·20
experienced	1·80	2·38

    Helpers increase the average number of offspring reared by inexperienced breeding pairs compared to experienced breeding pairs by

    A   19%
    B   23%
    C   45%
    D   60%.

[END OF SECTION 1. NOW ATTEMPT THE QUESTIONS IN SECTION 2 OF YOUR QUESTION AND ANSWER BOOKLET]

FOR OFFICIAL USE

AH
National Qualifications 2016

Mark

X707/77/01

Biology
Section 1 — Answer Grid and Section 2

MONDAY, 9 MAY

9:00 AM – 11:30 AM

Fill in these boxes and read what is printed below.

Full name of centre

Town

Forename(s)

Surname

Number of seat

Date of birth

Day   Month   Year

Scottish candidate number

Total marks — 90

SECTION 1 — 25 marks

Attempt ALL questions.

Instructions for completion of Section 1 are given on *Page two*.

SECTION 2 — 65 marks

Attempt ALL questions.

A Supplementary Sheet for Question 1 is enclosed inside the front cover of this question paper. Write your answers clearly in the spaces provided in this booklet. Additional space for answers and rough work is provided at the end of this booklet. If you use this space you must clearly identify the question number you are attempting. Any rough work must be written in this booklet. You should score through your rough work when you have written your final copy.

Use **blue** or **black** ink.

Before leaving the examination room you must give this booklet to the Invigilator; if you do not you may lose all the marks for this paper.

SQA

SECTION 1 — 25 marks

The questions for Section 1 are contained in the question paper X707/77/02.

Read these and record your answers on the answer grid on *Page three* opposite.

Use **blue** or **black** ink. Do NOT use gel pens or pencil.

1. The answer to each question is **either** A, B, C or D. Decide what your answer is, then fill in the appropriate bubble (see sample question below).

2. There is **only one correct** answer to each question.

3. Any rough working should be done on the additional space for answers and rough work at the end of this booklet.

Sample Question

The thigh bone is called the

    A   humerus

    B   femur

    C   tibia

    D   fibula.

The correct answer is **B** — femur. The answer **B** bubble has been clearly filled in (see below).

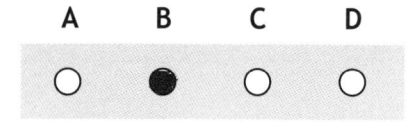

Changing an answer

If you decide to change your answer, cancel your first answer by putting a cross through it (see below) and fill in the answer you want. The answer below has been changed to **D**.

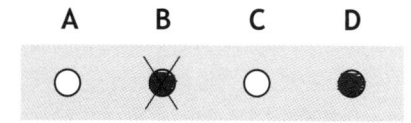

If you then decide to change back to an answer you have already scored out, put a tick (✓) to the **right** of the answer you want, as shown below:

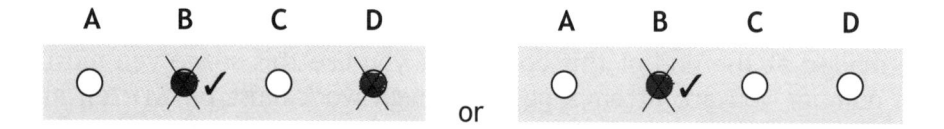

SECTION 1 — Answer Grid

[BLANK PAGE]

[Turn over for next question

DO NOT WRITE ON THIS PAGE

SECTION 2 — 65 marks

Attempt ALL questions

It should be noted that question 11 contains a choice.

1. Read through the Supplementary Sheet for Question 1 before attempting this question.

    (a) **Refer to Figure 2 in the Supplementary Sheet for Question 1.**

    (i) Use the data to describe the egg-laying of uninfected mosquitoes. **2**

    (ii) If the box plots were perfectly symmetrical, mean values for egg-laying would be very close to median values.

    State what can be deduced about the **mean** number of eggs laid by infected mosquitoes in relation to the median value. **1**

    (iii) Describe the effect that *Plasmodium* infection has on the fecundity of mosquitoes used in the study. **1**

    (b) **Refer to Figure 3 in the Supplementary Sheet for Question 1.**

    (i) The data shows that infection by *Plasmodium* appears to increase the longevity of female mosquitoes.

    Explain why the difference between the two groups can be regarded as significant. **1**

    (ii) Suggest a benefit to the parasite of its vector living longer. **1**

1. (continued)

    (c) **Refer to Figure 4 in the Supplementary Sheet for Question 1.**

        (i) Explain what the lines of best fit indicate about the relationship between longevity and fecundity in both infected and uninfected mosquitoes. **2**

        (ii) State, with justification, whether or not this data is reliable. **1**

[Turn over

2. Scientists have reported that neurons produced in cell culture from human stem cells have the potential to function when grafted into the site of a spinal injury in rats.

(a) State why the cell culture medium in which the neurons were cultured should contain serum.

(b) Scientists used a haemocytometer to perform a cell count to calculate the number of stem cells that developed into neurons.

The diagram below represents a sample from a culture placed in a haemocytometer and viewed under a microscope.

The grid is **0·1 mm** in depth.

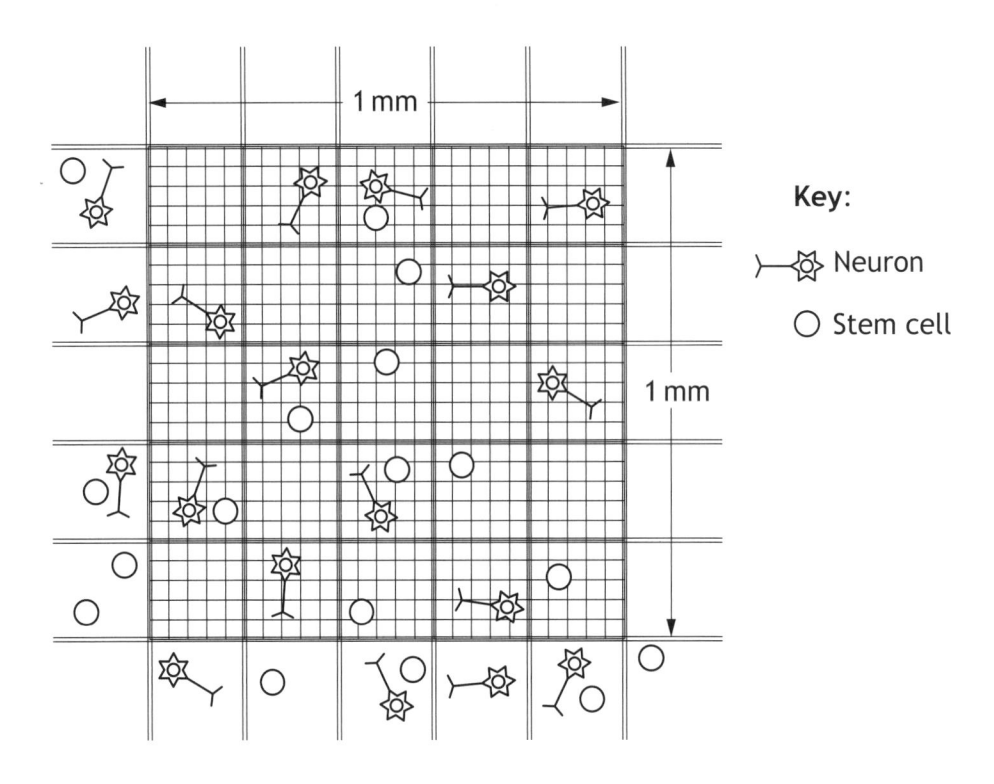

(i) Calculate the number of **neurons** in 1 cm³ of the culture.

Space for calculation

_____ neurons

(ii) Suggest **one** disadvantage of cell counts performed using the haemocytometer.

2. (continued)

(c) Bright field microscopy was used to view the cells grafted into the site of spinal injury.

State another type of biological material that can be viewed using bright field microscopy. **1**

_____

(d) In studies involving animals, state **one** way in which harm to the animals can be minimised. **1**

_____

[Turn over

3. Multiple sclerosis (MS) is a neurological condition in which the body's immune system destroys the myelin sheath that surrounds and insulates nerve axons.

A clinical study was carried out into the effects of a new drug *interferon beta-1b* for this condition. A randomised trial, with a negative control group (placebo), was carried out across four different health centres. During the study patients were given one of three treatments: 0·00 mg (placebo), 0·05 mg or 0·25 mg interferon. The patients administered the drug themselves at home.

The study measured how effective the drug was by asking patients to record any worsening of symptoms after 2 years of treatment. The study involved 372 patients aged 18-50 years. Fourteen patients dropped out before completing the trial.

Patients' results are shown in Table 1.

Table 1

Level of interferon beta-1b in treatment (mg)	Proportion of patients reporting no worsening of symptoms after 2 years of treatment (%)
0·00	16
0·05	18
0·25	25

At one health centre 52 patients were MRI scanned every 6 weeks to monitor any new damage to nerve tissue. The results are shown in Table 2.

Table 2

Level of interferon beta-1b in treatment (mg)	Proportion of patients showing new nerve damage (%)
0·00	29
0·05	no data recorded
0·25	6

(a) Identify the independent variable in this trial. 1

(b) This trial was carried out *in vivo*.

State **one** advantage of this type of trial. 1

3. (continued)

(c) Explain why a placebo group was included in this trial. **1**

(d) Suggest **one** way in which the results of the trial may not be reliable. **1**

(e) Describe an ethical issue that the researchers would need to consider before this trial. **1**

(f) Suggest **two** conclusions that can be drawn from the results of this trial. **2**

Conclusion 1 _____

Conclusion 2 _____

[Turn over

4. Sickle cell anaemia is an inherited blood disorder that reduces the ability of red blood cells to transport oxygen round the body by changing the structure of haemoglobin.

In sickle cell anaemia, the primary structure of a haemoglobin subunit is altered; the amino acid glutamic acid is substituted by the amino acid valine.

The structures of glutamic acid and valine are shown below.

(a) State the class of amino acids to which valine belongs. **1**

(b) Identify **one** type of secondary structure shown in the haemoglobin molecule in the figure below. **1**

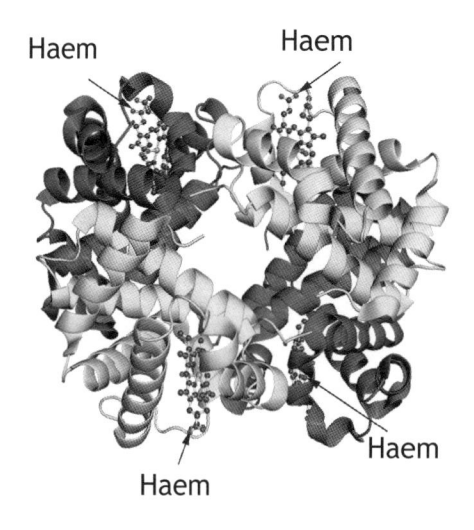

4. (continued)

(c) Explain the term cooperativity in relation to oxygen binding to haemoglobin.

(d) The graph below shows the oxygen saturation of haemoglobin at different oxygen pressures for an individual with normal haemoglobin and for another individual with sickle cell haemoglobin.

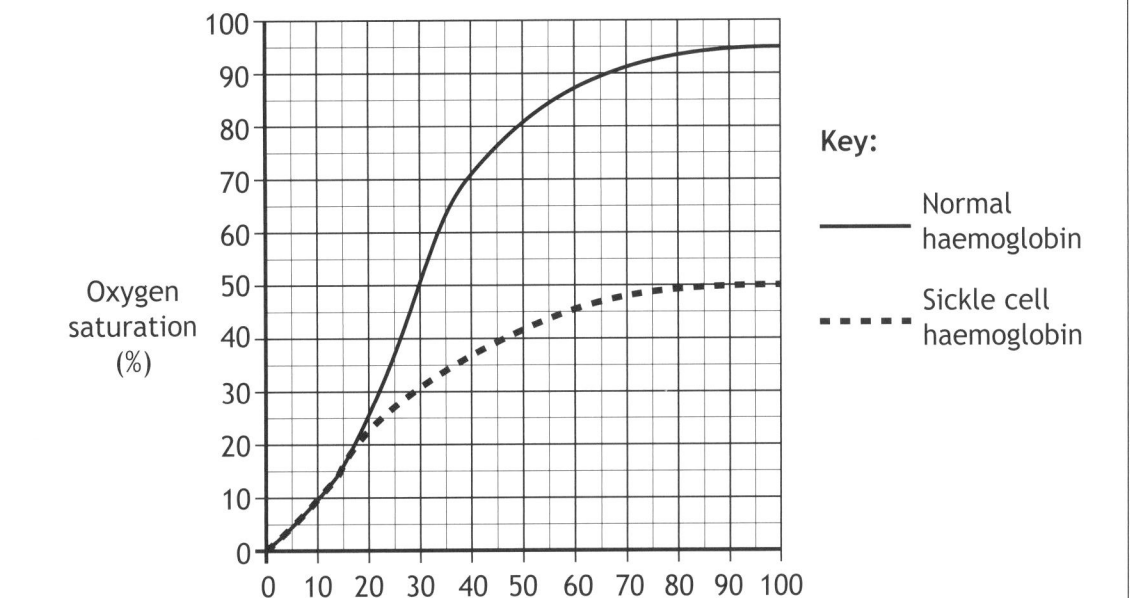

Use the graph to compare the oxygen saturation of normal and sickle cell haemoglobin as oxygen pressure increases.

(e) Molecules of sickle cell haemoglobin clump together preventing access to oxygen binding sites.

Suggest why this is a result of the substitution of glutamic acid by valine.

[Turn over

5. Describe the structure of spindle fibres and explain their role in the movement of chromosomes during cell division. **4**

6. The sodium potassium pump (Na/KATPase) is a membrane protein found in animal cells.

(a) Give **one** function of sodium potassium pumps.

(b) Describe the role of ATP in altering the affinity of the pump for sodium ions (Na$^+$).

(c) Digoxin is a chemical that inhibits the sodium potassium pump by binding to the potassium ion (K$^+$) binding site as shown in the diagram below.

Explain why binding by digoxin prevents further binding of sodium (Na$^+$) ions by the pump.

[Turn over

7. Binding of antidiuretic hormone (ADH) to its receptor on the plasma membrane of kidney collecting duct cells triggers the recruitment of water channel proteins as shown below.

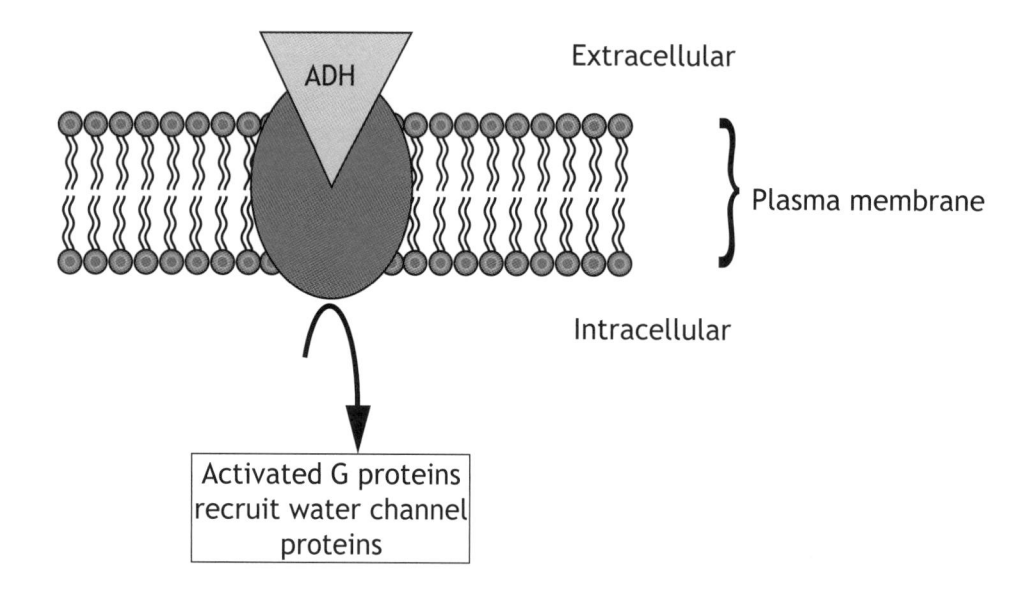

(a) (i) Name the water channel protein involved in this process.

(ii) Name the process by which a response within the cell is triggered by the binding of ADH to its cell surface receptor.

7. (continued)

(b) A urine output of greater than 0·05 litres per kg body mass per day is considered diagnostic of diabetes insipidus. The bar chart below shows the urine output over 6 days of a 70 kg individual being investigated for diabetes insipidus. During days 3 and 4 the individual was treated with the drug *desmopressin*, a synthetic form of ADH.

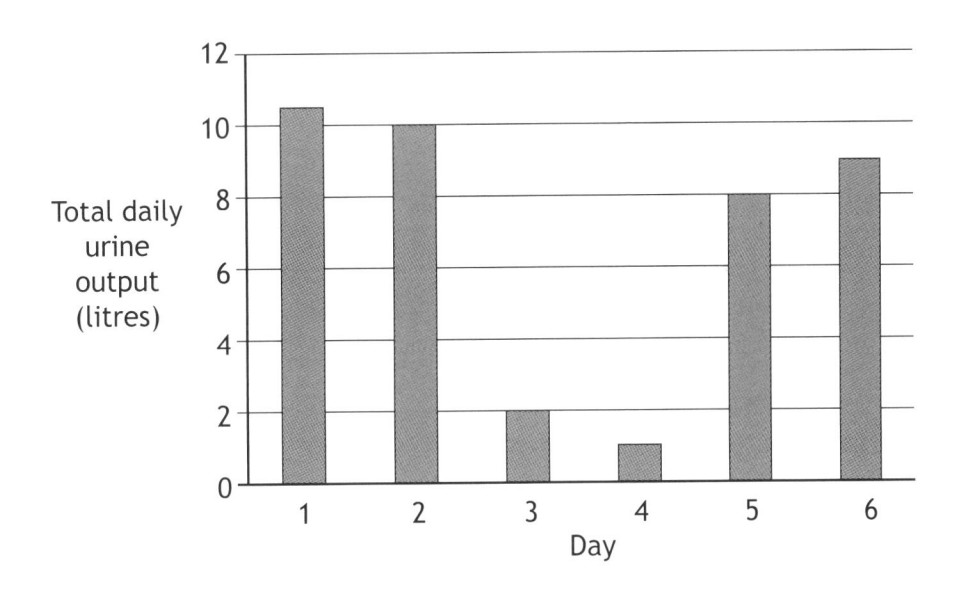

(i) Use the data to confirm that a diagnosis of diabetes insipidus is correct for this individual.

Space for calculation

(ii) Give evidence from the graph that supports the conclusion that *desmopressin* is an effective treatment.

(iii) Diabetes insipidus results from failure to recruit water channel proteins to the cell membrane.

Identify the cause of recruitment failure in this individual.

8. The diagram below shows the pairing of homologous chromosomes in a cell undergoing meiosis.

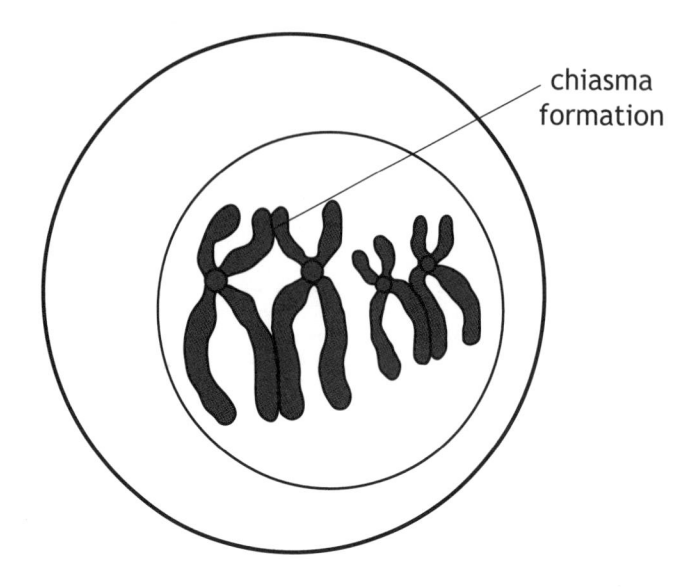

(a) Name the type of cell that undergoes meiosis. 1

(b) (i) Explain how the chiasma formation between the paired homologous chromosomes shown in the diagram leads to variation. 2

(ii) Name the process that ensures haploid gametes produced by meiosis contain a mixture of chromosomes of maternal and paternal origin. 1

[Turn over for next question

DO NOT WRITE ON THIS PAGE

9. In 1971, biologists moved five adult pairs of Italian wall lizards (*Podarcis sicula*) from their small home island of Kopiste to the neighbouring small island of Mrcaru, which did not have a lizard population. On their return in 2005 Mrcaru was found to have a large population of *P. sicula* (confirmed by genetic analysis) with significantly larger heads and a greater bite force than the lizards from Kopiste. Their digestive systems were also found to contain microorganisms that assist in the breakdown of plant cell walls.

The summer diets of the two lizard populations are shown below.

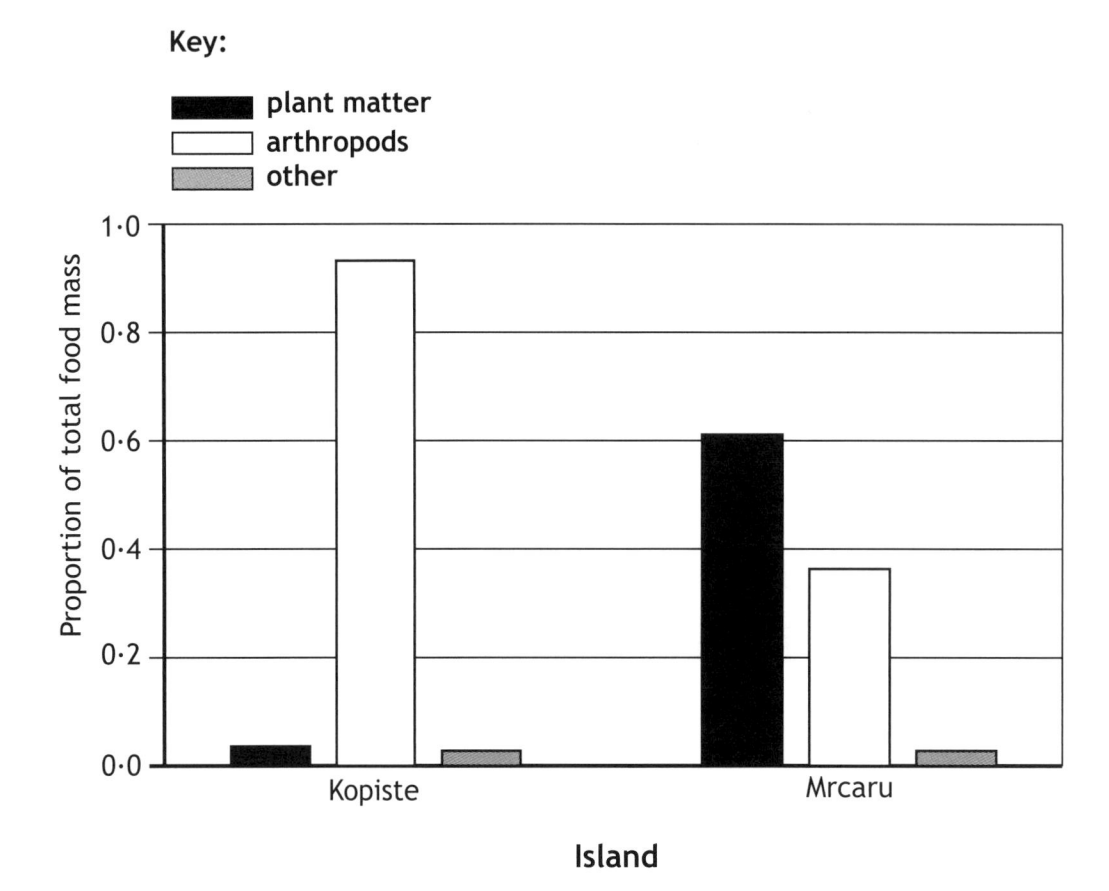

(a) Describe the most significant change in the summer diet of the lizards on Mrcaru. 1

9. (continued)

   (b) (i) Explain how the information supports the conclusion that the changes to the lizard population on Mrcaru were the result of natural selection. **2**

   (ii) Evolution of the lizards on Mrcaru occurred very rapidly.

   State **one** factor that can increase the rate of evolution. **1**

   (c) This study involved taking representative samples of the lizard populations on the two islands.

   State **one** feature of a representative sample. **1**

[Turn over

10. The Figures below show male and female capercaillies (*Tetrao urogallus*) which are found in some Scottish pine forests. Males are much larger and darker than females and the breast feathers of the male have a metallic green sheen.

male capercaillie

female capercaillie

(a) State the term used to indicate the different body forms of males and females belonging to this species.

(b) Capercaillies are a lekking species. Males perform displays during which they fan their tails, hold their wings down and make a variety of sounds. These features, which are attractive to females, are thought to serve as honest signals.

(i) Explain what is meant by a lekking species.

(ii) Explain why this display is often given as an example of sexual selection.

(iii) If the display provides honest signals, state the benefit that may be obtained by females receiving these signals.

10. (continued)

(c) Peacocks are the males of another lekking bird species, *Pavo cristatus*, whose natural habitat is the dense forests of South-East Asia. As well as the visual stimulus of a tail-feather display, peacocks, during mating, can emit a distinctive "hoot". These hoots are loud enough to be heard by other females, out of sight of the lek, who may be attracted by the calls and provide the dominant males at the lek with additional mating partners.

(i) Suggest why auditory stimuli are advantageous to species inhabiting forest ecosystems.

(ii) Recent research has found that some peacocks emit hoots in the complete absence of females at the lek. Females are still attracted to the lek by these sounds. Such "solo" hoots have been described as "dishonest signals".

Explain what is meant by a "dishonest signal" in this behaviour.

[Turn over for next question

11. Answer **either A or B** in the space below and on *Page twenty-five*.

    A Discuss reproduction under the following headings:

        (i) costs and benefits of sexual reproduction;   4

        (ii) asexual reproduction as a successful reproductive strategy.   5

OR

    B Discuss endoparasitic infections under the following headings:

        (i) difficulties involved in their treatment and control;   7

        (ii) benefits of improved parasite control to human populations.   2

Labelled diagrams may be used where appropriate.

SPACE FOR ANSWER FOR QUESTION 11

[END OF QUESTION PAPER]

ADDITIONAL SPACE FOR ANSWERS AND ROUGH WORK

National Qualifications 2016

X707/77/11

Biology
Supplementary Sheet

MONDAY, 9 MAY
9:00 AM – 11:30 AM

Supplementary Sheet for Question 1

1. Malaria is caused by unicellular parasites in the genus *Plasmodium*. Figure 1 shows the life cycle of the parasite with respect to its human and mosquito hosts.

    Figure 1

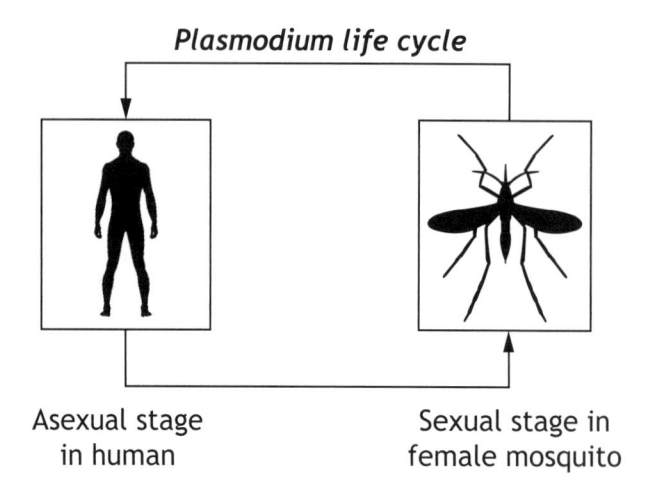

    Plasmodium life cycle

    Asexual stage in human   Sexual stage in female mosquito

    Malaria is a well-researched tropical disease of humans, but less is known about the effects of the parasite on its mosquito vector.

    The parasite *Plasmodium relictum* causes malaria in birds. A recent study has been carried out to investigate the effects of this parasite on the mosquito *Culex pipiens*. In particular, two aspects were investigated: fecundity (number of eggs laid) and longevity (measured as survival after egg laying) of the mosquitoes.

    In Figure 2, box-and-whisker plots show the total egg production by large numbers of uninfected and infected female mosquitoes.

    Figure 2

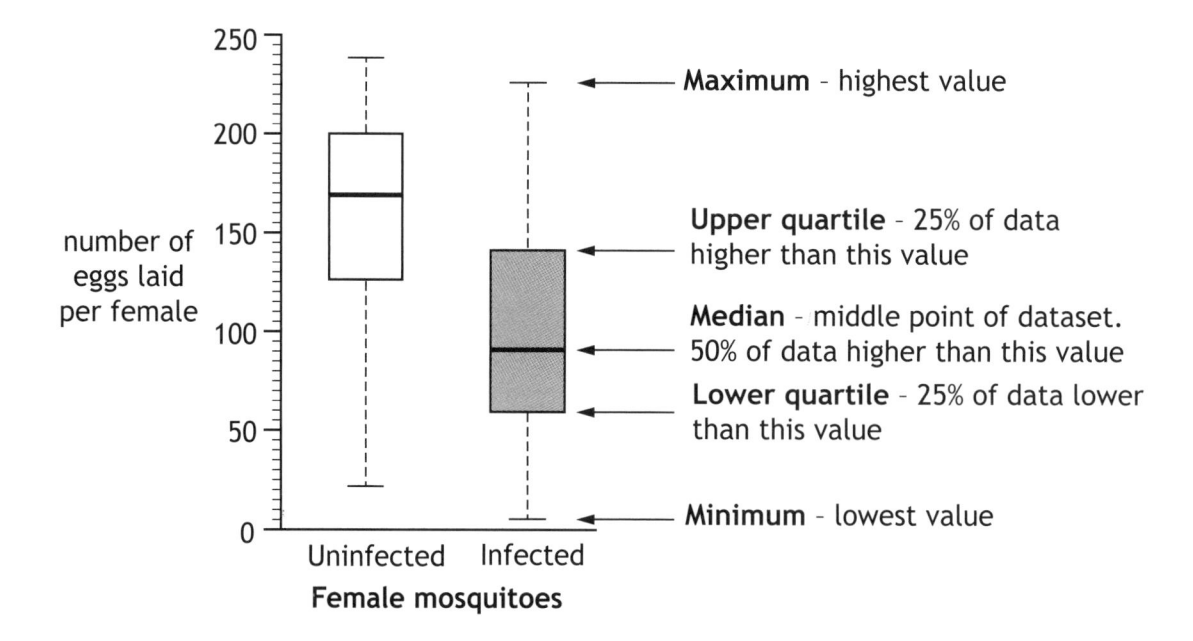

    Maximum – highest value

    Upper quartile – 25% of data higher than this value

    Median – middle point of dataset. 50% of data higher than this value

    Lower quartile – 25% of data lower than this value

    Minimum – lowest value

1. (continued)

Figure 3 shows mean survival times after egg laying for uninfected and infected female mosquitoes.

Figure 3

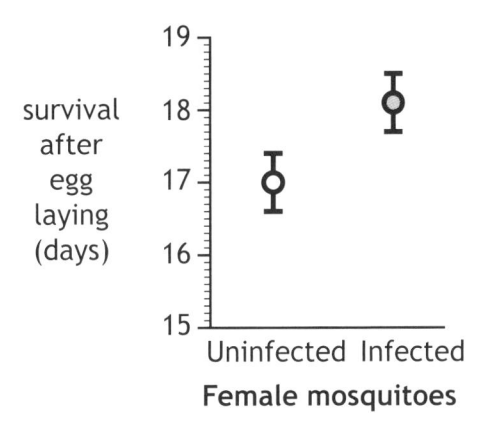

y-axis: survival after egg laying (days), from 15 to 19
x-axis: Female mosquitoes — Uninfected (~17), Infected (~18)

Fecundity and longevity were measured in the same individual female mosquitoes to see if there was a relationship between the two variables.

The lines of best fit for mosquito survival against the number of eggs each female laid were plotted for uninfected females and infected females.

This data is shown in Figure 4.

Figure 4

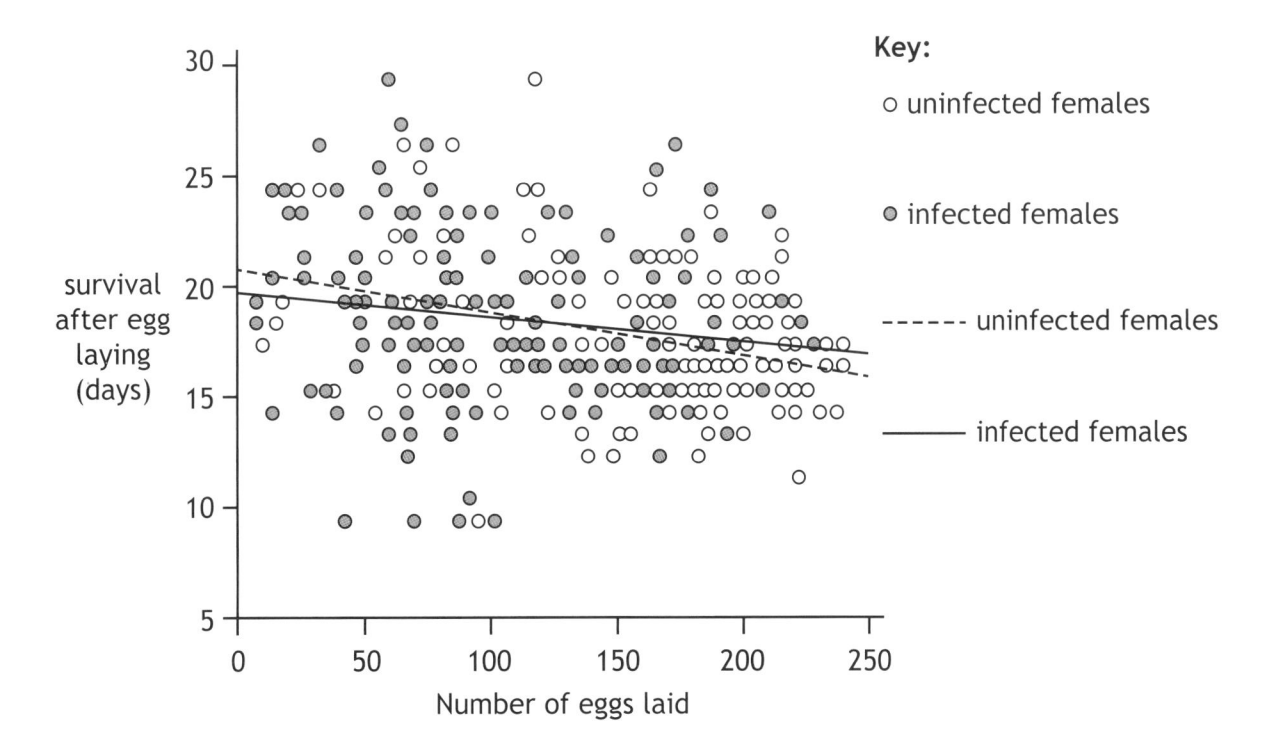

y-axis: survival after egg laying (days), from 5 to 30
x-axis: Number of eggs laid, from 0 to 250

Key:
○ uninfected females
● infected females
------ uninfected females
——— infected females

ADVANCED HIGHER
2017

National Qualifications 2017

X707/77/02

**Biology
Section 1 — Questions**

TUESDAY, 23 MAY
9:00 AM – 11:30 AM

Instructions for the completion of Section 1 are given on *Page two* of your question and answer booklet X707/77/01.

Record your answers on the answer grid on *Page three* of your question and answer booklet.

Before leaving the examination room you must give your question and answer booklet to the Invigilator; if you do not, you may lose all the marks for this paper.

SECTION 1 — 25 marks
Attempt ALL questions

1. Trypan blue is used as a vital stain to identify viable cells when viewed in a haemocytometer. A vital stain

   A   stains all cells
   B   only stains dead cells
   C   only stains living cells
   D   only stains the culture medium.

2. Bovine insulin is a soluble protein with an isoelectric point of pH 5·4.

   Which of the following graphs represents the level of precipitate formed as the pH of a bovine insulin solution is changed?

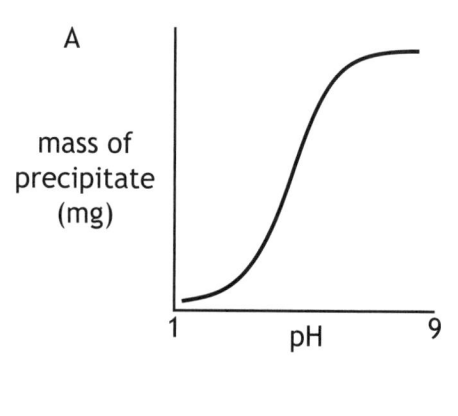

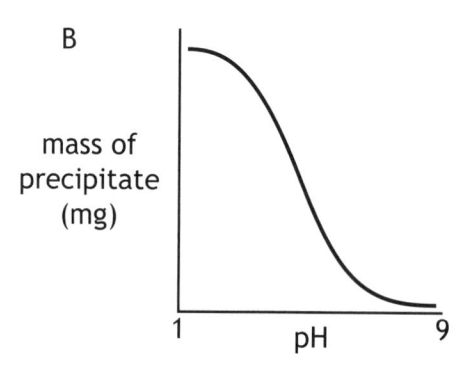

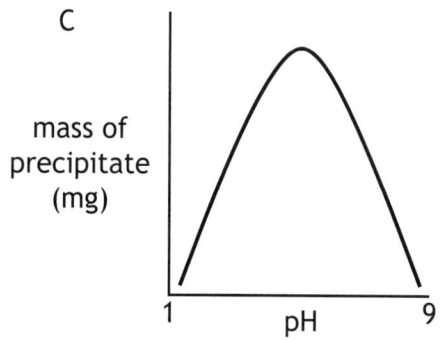

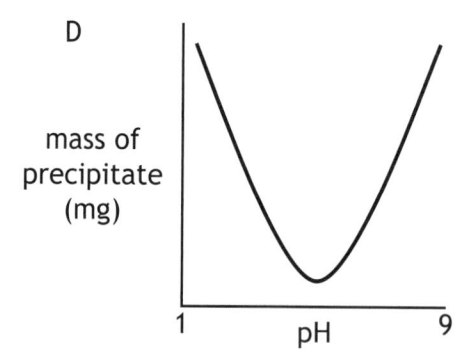

3. The figure shows how a scientist used serial dilution followed by plating to check the number of bacteria in a stock culture.

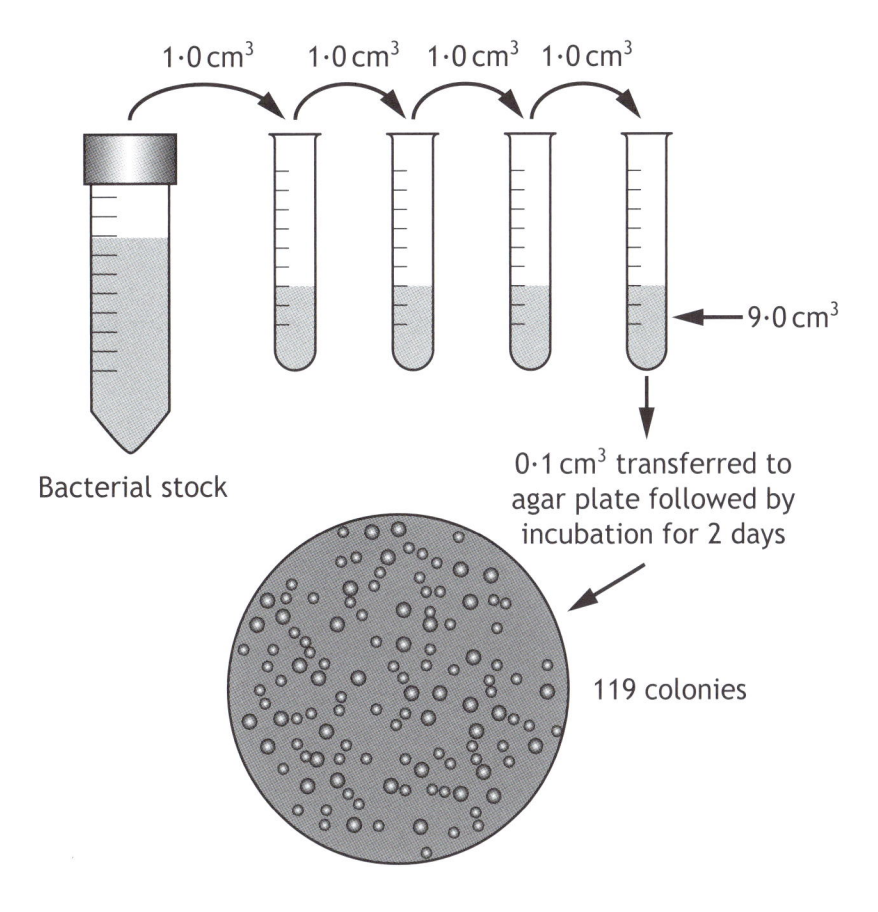

How many bacteria were there in 1 cm³ of the original bacterial stock?

A 1.19×10^5

B 1.19×10^6

C 1.19×10^7

D 1.19×10^8

4. Place the following events for a sodium potassium pump into the correct sequence.

1 Phosphorylation

2 Potassium ions released into cell

3 Transporter protein has high affinity for sodium ions inside the cell

4 Dephosphorylation

A 2, 1, 4, 3

B 3, 4, 2, 1

C 2, 1, 3, 4

D 3, 1, 4, 2

[Turn over

5. The binding of oxygen to haemoglobin is affected by small changes in temperature or pH.

   Which of the following changes would **decrease** haemoglobin's affinity for oxygen?

   A increased temperature, decreased pH

   B increased temperature, increased pH

   C decreased temperature, decreased pH

   D decreased temperature, increased pH

6. The gene represented in the diagram codes for multiple proteins due to alternative RNA splicing.

   The coding regions (exons) are labelled 1 to 10.

   Alternative RNA splicing results in an mRNA that contains exon 2 or 3, exon 4, 5 or 6 and exon 7 or 8.

   Predict the total number of different proteins that can be produced from this gene.

   A 3
   B 7
   C 12
   D 15

7. In an immunoassay used to detect the presence of an antigen for a disease-causing organism (pathogen), the following samples were tested.

   1   A sample from an individual thought to be infected with the pathogen.
   2   A sample from an organism known to cause similar symptoms, but unrelated to the pathogen.
   3   A sample from the pathogen.
   4   A sample of purified water.

   Which row in the table identifies the purpose of each sample?

	Positive control	Negative control	Test assay
A	3	4	2
B	3	2	1
C	2	4	3
D	2	3	1

8. Which of the following diagrams represents the sequence of phases involved in the cell cycle?

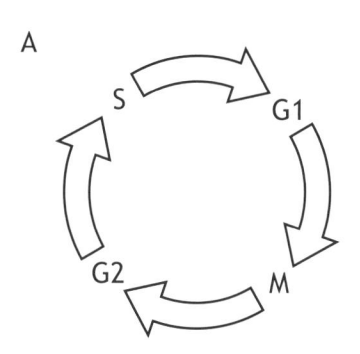

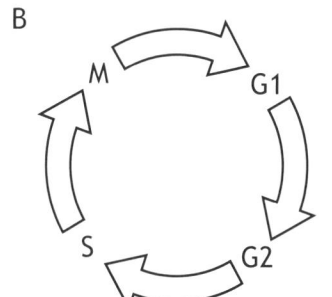

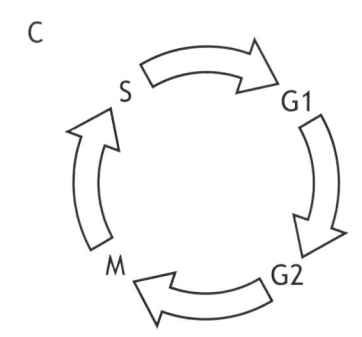

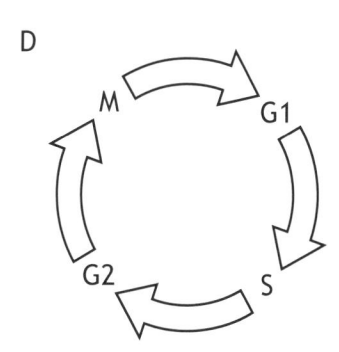

[Turn over

Page five

9. Which letter in the diagram represents the first stage in cell signalling for a peptide hormone molecule?

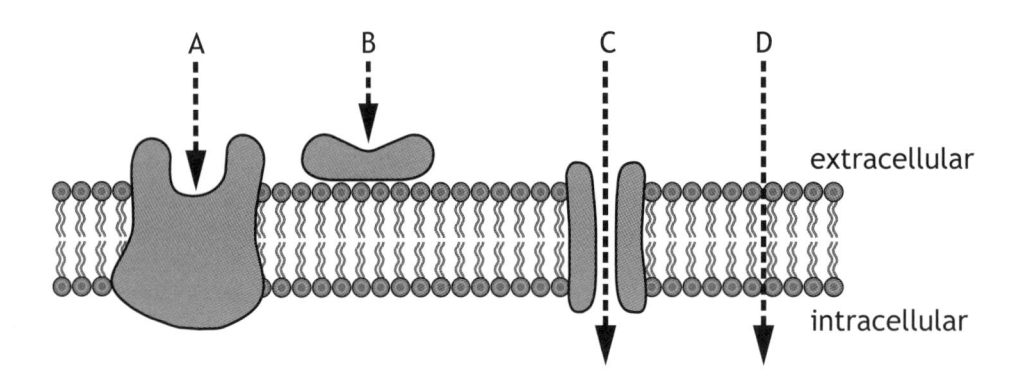

10. Red blood cells swell or shrink rapidly in response to changes in the water concentration around them. This is due to one type of water channel protein, Aquaporin 1 (AQP1).

    Each red blood cell can transport a total of 1×10^{14} water molecules per second and each AQP1 channel can transport 5×10^8 water molecules per second.

    How many AQP1 channels are present in the membrane of a red blood cell?

    A 2×10^5

    B 5×10^5

    C 2×10^6

    D 5×10^6

11. Which of the following changes in the rate of the cell cycle could result in a degenerative disease?

    A A controlled increase

    B A controlled decrease

    C An uncontrolled increase

    D An uncontrolled decrease

12. Which of the following diagrams represents the sequence of stages involved in mitosis?

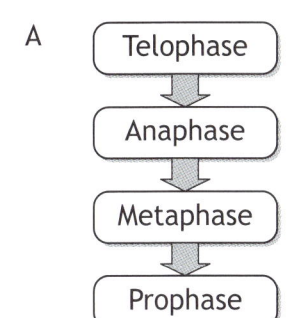

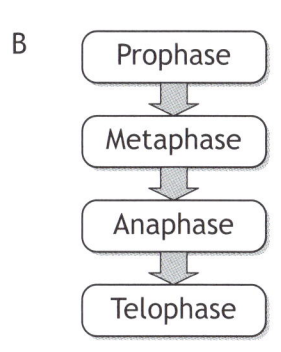

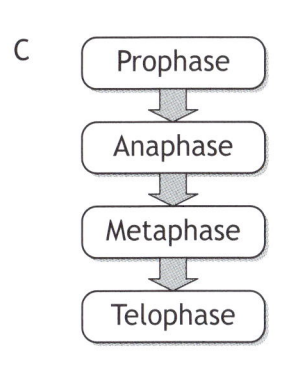

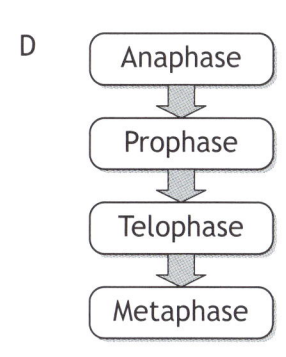

A Telophase → Anaphase → Metaphase → Prophase

B Prophase → Metaphase → Anaphase → Telophase

C Prophase → Anaphase → Metaphase → Telophase

D Anaphase → Prophase → Telophase → Metaphase

13. Bacteriophage M13 is a virus that can infect bacteria. When bacteria in the lab are infected with M13, it is essential to use the correct ratio of one virus particle to two bacterial cells.

A 0·25 cm³ sample of an *E. coli* culture having a concentration of 8×10^8 cells per cm³ is placed into a tube.

What volume of a bacteriophage stock having a concentration of 2×10^9 bacteriophage per cm³ should be added to the cell sample to give a bacteriophage to bacteria ratio of 1:2?

A   0·05 cm³

B   0·2 cm³

C   5 cm³

D   20 cm³

[Turn over

14. A student planned to measure the activity of catalase by using an oxygen probe to measure oxygen production. As part of their pilot study, the student used a standard sample with an oxygen concentration of 22·00% to test the accuracy and precision of the probe.

Four readings of the standard sample were taken and the results obtained are shown in the table.

	Reading			
	1	2	3	4
Oxygen concentration (%)	20·94	20·93	20·93	20·94

The results indicate the measurements taken were

A accurate and precise

B accurate but not precise

C precise but not accurate

D neither accurate nor precise.

15. Which of the following formulae would allow relative fitness to be calculated?

A $\dfrac{\text{frequency of a particular genotype after selection}}{\text{frequency of a particular genotype before selection}}$

B $\dfrac{\text{frequency of a particular genotype before selection}}{\text{frequency of a particular genotype after selection}}$

C $\dfrac{\text{number of surviving offspring of a particular genotype}}{\text{number of surviving offspring of other genotypes}}$

D $\dfrac{\text{number of surviving offspring of other genotypes}}{\text{number of surviving offspring of a particular genotype}}$

16. Some invertebrate species can be used as indicator species to assess the level of pollution by organic waste in freshwater systems. Species within the taxa *Ephemeroptera* (mayflies), *Plecoptera* (stoneflies) and *Trichoptera* (caddisflies) are particularly sensitive to pollution. These taxa are referred to collectively as EPT taxa.

The presence of these species can be used to assess water pollution levels by calculating an EPT index using the formula shown. The value obtained allows the water quality to be assessed using Table 1.

$$\text{EPT index} = \frac{\text{total number of EPT taxa present} \times 100}{\text{total number of taxa present}}$$

Table 1

EPT index	Water quality
>50%	excellent
35-49%	good
25-34%	moderate
<25%	poor

A study sampled the invertebrate species in a stretch of river and the results are shown in Table 2.

Table 2

Taxa	Number of individuals
Striped stonefly	6
Dragonfly	5
Simulid blackfly	9
Net-spinning caddisfly	6
Bloodworm	8
Flathead mayfly	3
Damselfly	7

The data suggests the water quality of this river is

A excellent

B good

C moderate

D poor.

[Turn over

17. The smaller tea tortrix (*Adoxophyes honmai*) is a moth that is an economically important pest of tea plants in Japan. *A honmai* has a number of development stages (larvae) from egg to adult.

Viruses that infect crop pests have potential use in controlling pest populations. A study compared the infection and killing of *A honmai* by two viruses, X and Y. Mean survival time after infection for each larval stage was measured and the results are shown in the table. Uninfected larvae were then released onto tea plants that had either virus X, virus Y or no virus applied to their leaves. The percentage infection of the larvae was measured and the results are shown in the graph.

Stage of insect development when infected	Mean survival time ± SE (days)	
	Virus X infection	Virus Y infection
1st	18·9 ± 0·6	5·8 ± 0·1
2nd	15·2 ± 0·4	7·0 ± 0·1
3rd	12·2 ± 0·2	7·0 ± 0·1
4th	10·1 ± 0·2	8·0 ± 0·1
5th	8·0 ± 0·1	6·9 ± 0·1

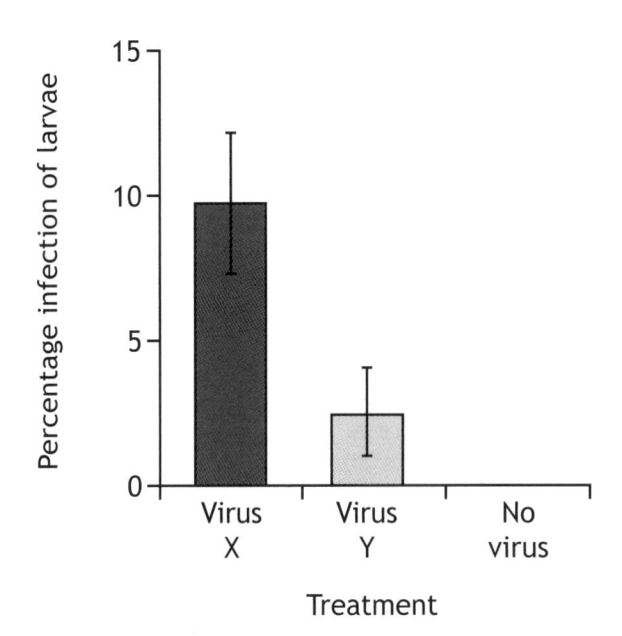

Which of the following conclusions can be drawn from this information?

A   Virus X has a higher transmission rate and is more virulent than Virus Y.

B   Virus X has a higher transmission rate and is less virulent than Virus Y.

C   Virus X has a lower transmission rate and is less virulent than Virus Y.

D   Virus X has a lower transmission rate and is more virulent than Virus Y.

18. Parthenogenesis is most likely to be common in environments with a

    A   warm climate and low parasite density

    B   warm climate and high parasite density

    C   cool climate and low parasite density

    D   cool climate and high parasite density.

19. Asexual reproduction is most likely to be a successful reproductive strategy in

    A   wide, stable niches

    B   narrow, stable niches

    C   wide, unstable niches

    D   narrow, unstable niches.

20. The black grouse male is larger and more brightly coloured than the female and competes with other males at leks.

Which of the following pairs of features are characteristic of this species?

    A   Monogamy and sexual dimorphism

    B   Monogamy and reversed sexual dimorphism

    C   Polygamy and sexual dimorphism

    D   Polygamy and reversed sexual dimorphism

21. Which of the following conversions is catalysed by reverse transcriptase?

    A   RNA → DNA

    B   RNA → protein

    C   DNA → RNA

    D   DNA → protein

[Turn over

22. The figure represents the structure of a Zika virus.

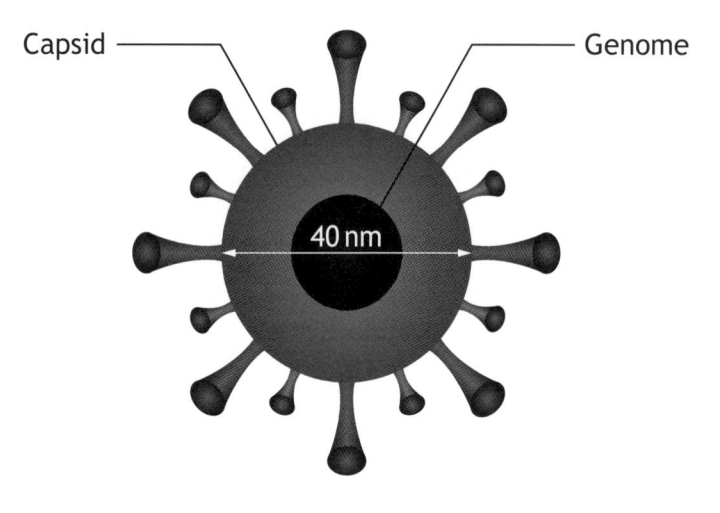

Capsid — Genome

40 nm

1,000,000 nm = 1 mm

Which row in the table describes the structure of a Zika virus?

	Capsid	Genome	Diameter (m)
A	Protein	Nucleic acid	40×10^{-6}
B	Protein	Nucleic acid	40×10^{-9}
C	Nucleic acid	Protein	40×10^{-6}
D	Nucleic acid	Protein	40×10^{-9}

23. Schistosomiasis in humans is caused by an

- A ectoparasitic arthropod
- B endoparasitic amoeba
- C endoparasitic nematode
- D endoparasitic platyhelminth.

24. Cholera is a disease which causes diarrhoea and is potentially fatal. It is transmitted through the consumption of food or water contaminated by the bacterium *Vibrio cholerae*. It often has a higher incidence in refugee camps than in the surrounding countryside.

Which of the following measures is **not** appropriate for reducing the incidence of cholera in refugee camps?

- A Improved vector control
- B Increased sanitation
- C Decreased population density
- D Reduced costs for cholera vaccines

25. The scatterplot shows the results obtained when life expectancy at birth was plotted against age at first reproduction for 24 species of mammals of different sizes.

Which of the following conclusions can be drawn from the data?

A An increase in life expectancy causes an increase in the age of first reproduction.

B An increase in the age of first reproduction causes an increase in life expectancy.

C Larger animals have longer life expectancy.

D Life expectancy and age at first reproduction are correlated.

[END OF SECTION 1. NOW ATTEMPT THE QUESTIONS IN SECTION 2 OF YOUR QUESTION AND ANSWER BOOKLET.]

National Qualifications 2017

FOR OFFICIAL USE

Mark

X707/77/01

Biology
Section 1 — Answer Grid and Section 2

TUESDAY, 23 MAY

9:00 AM – 11:30 AM

Fill in these boxes and read what is printed below.

Full name of centre

Town

Forename(s)

Surname

Number of seat

Date of birth
Day   Month   Year   Scottish candidate number

Total marks — 90

SECTION 1 — 25 marks

Attempt ALL questions.

Instructions for the completion of Section 1 are given on *Page two*.

SECTION 2 — 65 marks

Attempt ALL questions.

A Supplementary Sheet for Question 1 is enclosed inside the front cover of this question paper.

Write your answers clearly in the spaces provided in this booklet. Additional space for answers and rough work is provided at the end of this booklet. If you use this space you must clearly identify the question number you are attempting. Any rough work must be written in this booklet. You should score through your rough work when you have written your final copy.

Use **blue** or **black** ink.

Before leaving the examination room you must give this booklet to the Invigilator; if you do not, you may lose all the marks for this paper.

SQA

SECTION 1 — 25 marks

The questions for Section 1 are contained in the question paper X707/77/02.

Read these and record your answers on the answer grid on *Page three* opposite.

Use **blue** or **black** ink. Do NOT use gel pens or pencil.

1. The answer to each question is **either** A, B, C or D. Decide what your answer is, then fill in the appropriate bubble (see sample question below).

2. There is **only one correct** answer to each question.

3. Any rough working should be done on the additional space for answers and rough work at the end of this booklet.

Sample Question

The thigh bone is called the

    A humerus

    B femur

    C tibia

    D fibula.

The correct answer is **B** — femur. The answer **B** bubble has been clearly filled in (see below).

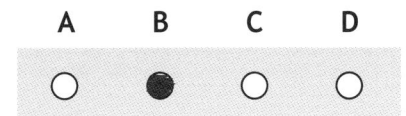

Changing an answer

If you decide to change your answer, cancel your first answer by putting a cross through it (see below) and fill in the answer you want. The answer below has been changed to **D**.

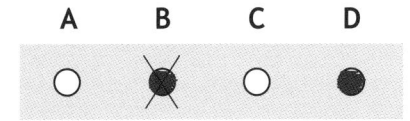

If you then decide to change back to an answer you have already scored out, put a tick (✓) to the **right** of the answer you want, as shown below:

SECTION 1 — Answer Grid

	A	B	C	D
1	○	○	○	○
2	○	○	○	○
3	○	○	○	○
4	○	○	○	○
5	○	○	○	○
6	○	○	○	○
7	○	○	○	○
8	○	○	○	○
9	○	○	○	○
10	○	○	○	○
11	○	○	○	○
12	○	○	○	○
13	○	○	○	○
14	○	○	○	○
15	○	○	○	○
16	○	○	○	○
17	○	○	○	○
18	○	○	○	○
19	○	○	○	○
20	○	○	○	○
21	○	○	○	○
22	○	○	○	○
23	○	○	○	○
24	○	○	○	○
25	○	○	○	○

[Turn over

[BLANK PAGE]

DO NOT WRITE ON THIS PAGE

[Turn over for next question

DO NOT WRITE ON THIS PAGE

SECTION 2 — 65 marks

Attempt ALL questions

It should be noted that question 11 contains a choice

1. Read through the Supplementary Sheet for Question 1 before attempting this question.

    (a) **Refer to Figure 2 in the Supplementary Sheet for Question 1.**

    Describe the trend shown in Figure 2. **1**

    (b) Describe the action of caspases in cell destruction. **1**

    (c) **Refer to Figure 3 in the Supplementary Sheet for Question 1.**

    (i) Explain how the data supports the conclusion that the intrinsic pathway for apoptosis is triggered by the extract. **2**

    (ii) Describe what the three negative values in Figure 3 indicate about the level of apoptosis in these treatments. **1**

1. (continued)

    (d) **Refer to Figures 4A and 4B in the Supplementary Sheet for Question 1.**

        (i) Calculate the percentage increase in the number of cells with 400 units of DNA in the cells treated with extract compared to the control cells.

        Space for calculation

        (ii) It was concluded that the extract initiated cell cycle arrest at a checkpoint after DNA replication but prior to cell division in these cells.

        Explain how the data in Figures 4A and 4B support this hypothesis.

[Turn over

Page seven

2. The light sensitive layer at the back of the human eye is called the retina. It is able to detect light due to the presence of photoreceptor cells called cones and rods. There are three types of cone cells (blue, green and red) which are sensitive to different wavelengths of light as shown in Figure 1. Different wavelengths of light are perceived as different colours.

Figure 1

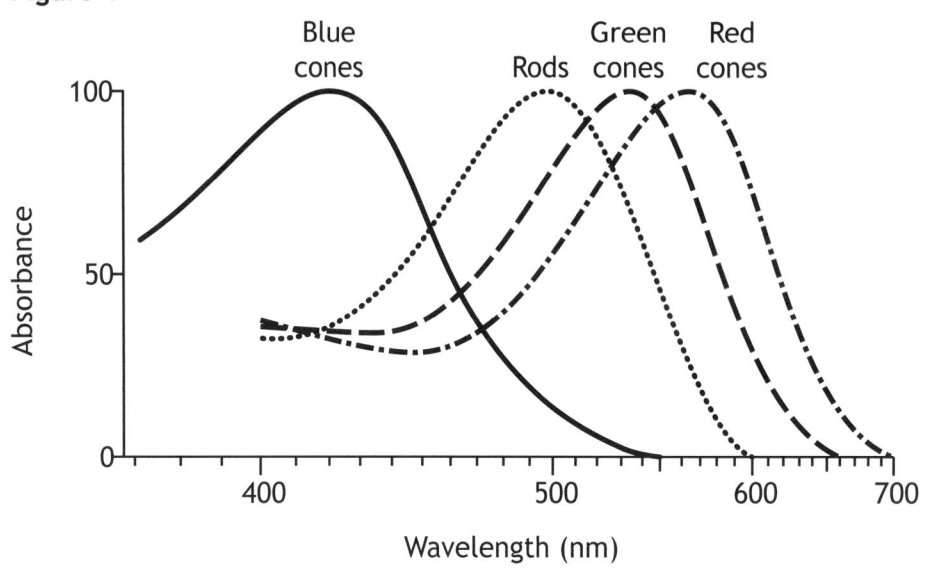

(a) (i) In cone cells, the light sensitive molecule retinal combines with a membrane protein to form photoreceptor proteins.

Name this membrane protein.

(ii) One percent of human males do not have functional red cone cells, a colour vision deficiency called *protanopia*.

Affected individuals would perceive a red object reflecting light of a wavelength of 670 nm as black.

Use Figure 1 to explain this observation.

2. (continued)

(b) Rod cells are more sensitive than cone cells at low light intensities.
State how this sensitivity is achieved. **1**

(c) Most birds have four types of cone cells.
Name the additional wavelength range to which these organisms are sensitive. **1**

[Turn over

3. Cortisol is a hydrophobic signalling molecule, produced by the human adrenal gland, that affects a number of different tissues in response to stress. It has a role in increasing blood sugar levels, in suppressing the immune system, and in promoting the metabolism of fats, proteins, and carbohydrates.

(a) (i) Cortisol is a steroid hormone.

Describe the mechanism by which this type of signalling molecule causes an effect within the target cell. **2**

(ii) Suggest a way in which cortisol might have different effects in different tissues. **1**

3. (continued)

(b) Addison's disease is a disorder in which the adrenal glands do not produce sufficient cortisol. One test for this disease is to give the patient an injection of a hormone called ACTH, which stimulates the adrenal gland to release cortisol. In a healthy person, cortisol levels should rise by at least 70 µg per litre after 30 minutes **and** 110 µg per litre after 60 minutes.

The graph shows the results of this test on three patients who were investigated for Addison's disease.

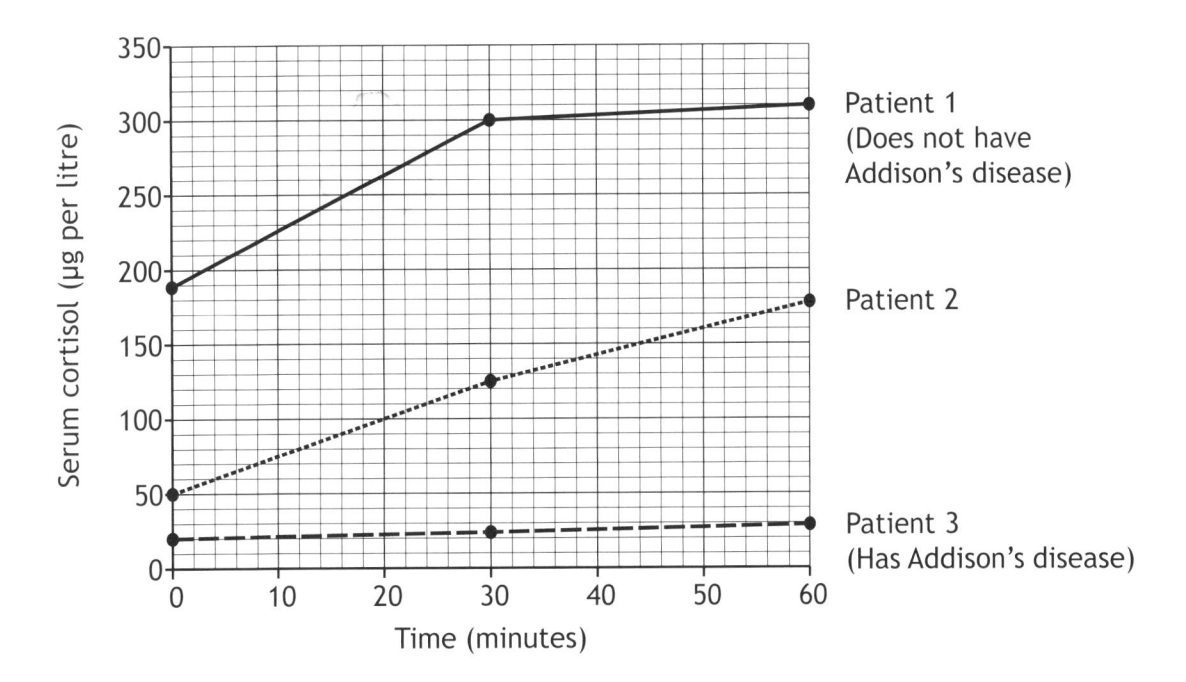

State the diagnosis that would be appropriate for Patient 2, using data to justify your answer.

1

[Turn over

4. The diagram shows how two types of enzyme can be involved in controlling the activity of a protein in response to the presence of a signalling molecule within the cell (intracellular signal molecule). Intracellular signalling molecules are often produced as a result of extracellular signals received by cell-surface receptors.

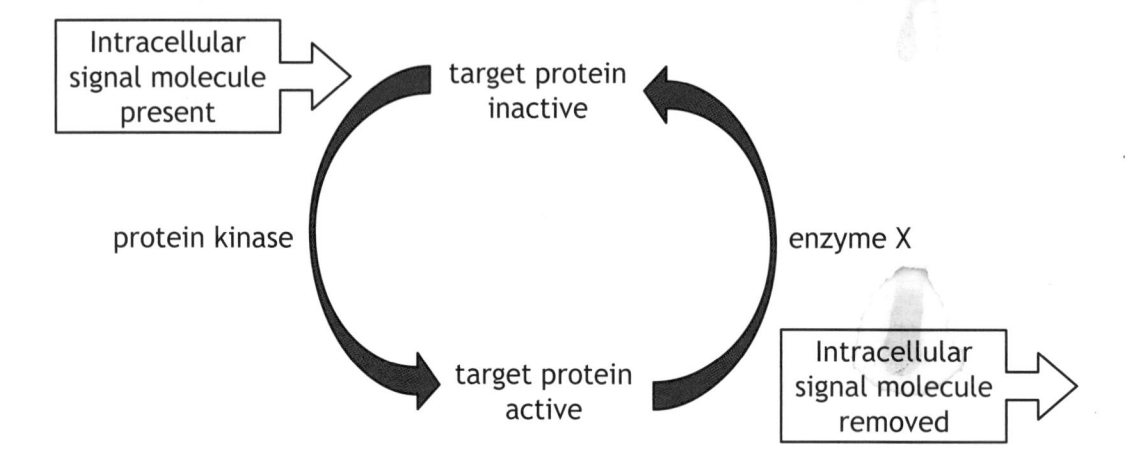

(a) (i) Explain how the action of protein kinase can switch a target protein from inactive to active. **1**

(ii) Name the type of enzyme represented by enzyme X. **1**

(iii) Explain the importance of the system being able to return the target protein to its inactive state. **1**

Page twelve

4. (continued)

(b) Protein kinase A (PKA) is an enzyme that is involved in this type of signalling. To test the hypothesis that PKA is found in a variety of cell types, cell extracts were prepared from different cell types and the proteins in the extracts separated by electrophoresis in a gel. The proteins were blotted onto a solid support and an antibody recognising PKA (anti-PKA antibody) was used to detect the presence of PKA.

(i) Describe how protein electrophoresis is used to separate proteins. **1**

(ii) Explain how the anti-PKA antibody would be used to detect the presence of PKA. **2**

[Turn over

5. The water vole (*Arvicola amphibius*) was common in Scotland but has declined markedly in recent years due to habitat loss and predation by American mink (*Neovison vison*).

A survey was carried out to estimate the population of water voles on a Scottish river system by counting the number of latrines (droppings sites) on a river bank at the water's edge. Water vole latrines are created as part of a territorial behaviour where a water vole will revisit the same site over and over again to deposit its droppings.

Water vole

American mink

(a) Suggest one reason why counting latrines is an appropriate indirect sampling technique for water voles.

(b) The survey team worked on a total of 518 km, using survey sites of 500 m at 5 km intervals along the river system. The number of latrines per kilometre of waterways was counted.

Name the type of sampling used.

5. (continued)

(c) All surveys were conducted in June, July and August of the same year. There was heavy rainfall for three days in August. Any survey site too deep to walk into was omitted. The remains of one water vole that had been preyed upon were discovered at one survey site. Of the 92 sites sampled, only one site showed any latrines.

Identify one aspect of the experimental design that shows:

(i) High reliability; 1

(ii) Low reliability. 1

(d) It was concluded that the water vole population on this river had become extremely low due to predation by American mink.

Give two reasons why this may **not** be a valid conclusion. 2

1 _____

2 _____

[Turn over

MARKS

6. The mechanism of sex determination is not the same for all species.

   (a) In most mammals the sex of the organism is determined by its genotype.

   Describe how genetic control determines the phenotype of maleness in **mammals**. **1**

   (b) In some reptile species the sex of offspring is environmentally rather than genetically controlled.

   Describe how an environmental factor can influence the sex ratio of offspring in such species. **1**

   (c) Diabetes insipidus is a condition characterised by the production of an excessive volume of dilute urine. An hereditary form of the disease in humans is the result of an X-linked mutation in the gene coding for the receptor for the hormone ADH. The mutated allele (X^a) is recessive to the normal allele (X^A).

   (i) Explain why males are more likely to be affected by diabetes insipidus than females. **1**

   (ii) Explain why carrier females are usually not affected by diabetes insipidus even though they carry a mutated copy of the gene. **2**

6. (c) (continued)

(iii) A man who is not affected by diabetes insipidus has a partner who is a carrier.

State the proportion of their sons that would be predicted to have the condition.

Space for working

_____ %

[Turn over

7. Students observed a group of California sea lions (*Zalophus californianus*) that were situated on a rocky outcrop off the coast of California. During each observation period, ten sea lions were observed for six minutes each. The sea lions were watched from a distance using binoculars. The checklist was used as a reference when recording the behaviours observed.

Behaviour	Description of behaviour
grooming	Licking, smoothing self with tongue, scratching
observing	Sitting up on flippers looking around
resting	Lying down with some head raising, barking or yawning
movement, aggressive	Barking, aggressive charging or chasing
movement, non-aggressive	Moving for better position on rock
other	Behaviours not specified above

California sea lion

(a) State the term used for a behavioural checklist of this kind. **1**

(b) As they observed the sea lions the students noted the time at which each new behaviour started.

Describe how the data could be used to construct a time budget. **1**

7. (continued)

   (c) One student noted, "Sometimes the sea lions tried to annoy each other."

   Explain why anthropomorphic statements such as this should be avoided in behavioural studies.

   1

   (d) Observing the sea lions from a distance made distinguishing some details of behaviour difficult.

   Suggest an improvement to the method, other than direct observation, that would reduce this source of error.

   1

   [Turn over

8. "So sex exists to keep parasites at bay." (Lane, 2009)

With reference to the Red Queen hypothesis, discuss the importance of sexual reproduction in defence against parasites.

5

[Turn over for next question

DO NOT WRITE ON THIS PAGE

9. *Acraea encedon* is a butterfly found in tropical Africa.

Females of this species can be one of two types: either producing broods that are entirely female or producing broods that have males and females in an approximate 1:1 sex ratio. One hypothesis proposed to explain the all-female broods was that bacteria inherited from the mother kill male embryos only.

(a) Explain how antibiotics that kill bacteria could be used in a controlled trial to test this hypothesis.

(b) Research has shown that the rapid evolution of male-killing bacteria from non-male-killing strains has been enabled by horizontal gene transfer.

Explain what is meant by "horizontal gene transfer".

9. (continued)

(c) Some populations of the butterfly are extremely female-biased with over 90% being infected with this bacterium. These females form lekking swarms at landmarks. This has been described as *sex-role-reversal*. Butterfly populations that are not female-biased do not have lekking swarms.

Suggest the purpose of the lekking swarms and explain why they are only found in female-biased populations of the butterfly. **2**

(d) Other sex-role-reversed mating systems are usually associated with males investing more than females in offspring, but this is not the case with *A. encedon*.

Suggest **one** way in which males might demonstrate greater reproductive investment than females in a sex-role-reversed mating system. **1**

[Turn over

10. The graph shows the number of measles notifications (reported cases) since 1950 and vaccination rates since 1970.

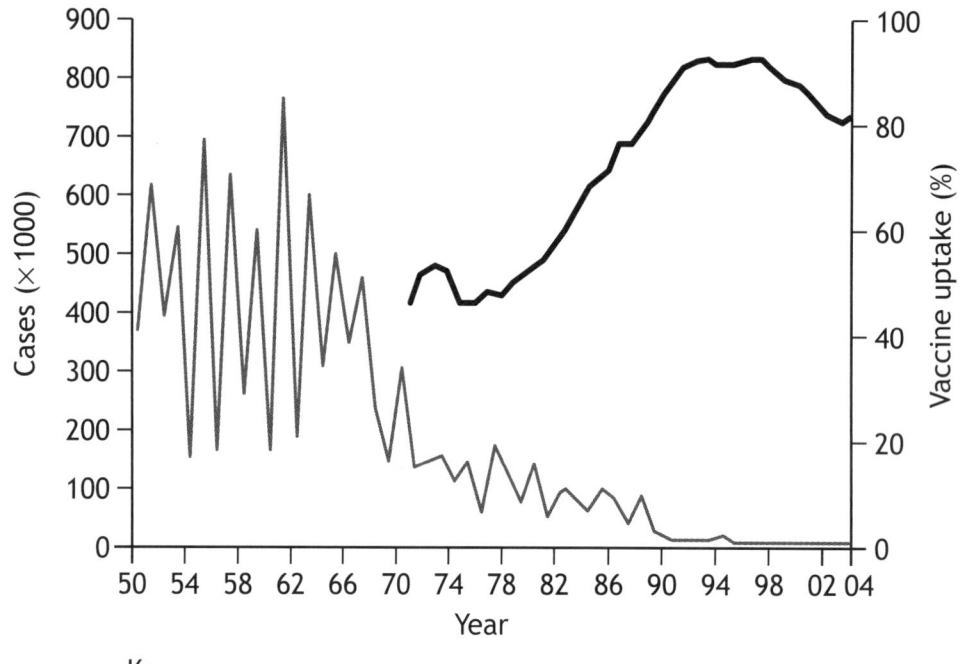

Key:
— Measles notification (×1000)
— Vaccine uptake (%)

(a) State the term used to describe the study of data concerned with the outbreak and spread of infectious disease. 1

(b) Describe the pattern of measles notifications prior to the introduction of vaccination. 1

(c) Describe the correlation suggested by the graph. 1

10. (continued)

(d) The MMR vaccine was introduced in 1988 to combat the infectious viral diseases of measles, mumps and rubella. In 1998, a report, published in a peer reviewed medical journal, claimed to establish a link between the MMR vaccine and the disorder known as autism.

(i) Explain what is meant by the term "peer reviewed". **1**

(ii) Although criticised heavily and eventually discredited, this research led to a considerable reduction in the number of children being vaccinated. In some areas, such as Swansea in South Wales, vaccination rates fell as low as 67·5%. Over the same period, a huge increase in the number of measles notifications occurred in that area.

Account for the spread of measles in the Swansea epidemic. **1**

(iii) Explain how the events in Swansea confirm that the graph not only shows correlation but also shows causation. **1**

(e) The World Health Organisation (WHO) recommends 95% of children should be immunised (vaccinated) against measles in order to protect all.

State the term used to describe this WHO threshold. **1**

[Turn over for next question

11. Answer **either A or B** in the space below and on *Page twenty-seven*.

    A Discuss the role of amino acid R-groups in:

        (i) the determination of tertiary structure of proteins;   **3**

        (ii) influencing the location of proteins within cells.   **6**

  OR

    B Discuss cell membranes under the following headings:

        (i) the phospholipid bilayer as a selective barrier;   **2**

        (ii) types of transport proteins and their functions.   **7**

SPACE FOR ANSWER FOR QUESTION 11

[END OF QUESTION PAPER]

ADDITIONAL SPACE FOR ANSWERS AND ROUGH WORK

AH

National Qualifications 2017

X707/77/11

Biology
Supplementary Sheet

TUESDAY, 23 MAY
9:00 AM – 11:30 AM

Supplementary Sheet for Question 1

1. There are two main pathways of programmed cell death (apoptosis): *intrinsic* (from within the cell) and *extrinsic* (from outside the cell).

   Figure 1 summarises some of the main features of the two pathways.

   Figure 1

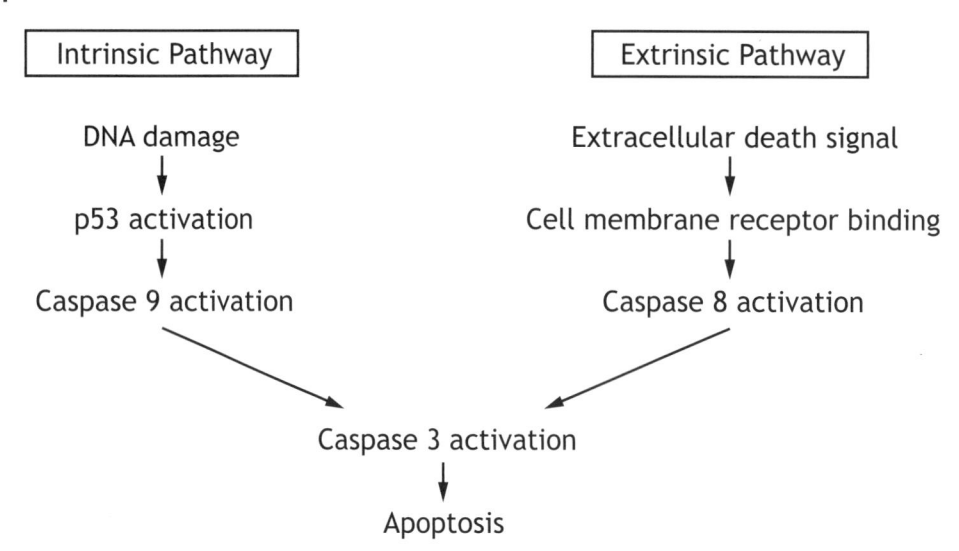

   ```
   Intrinsic Pathway                    Extrinsic Pathway

   DNA damage                           Extracellular death signal
        ↓                                        ↓
   p53 activation                       Cell membrane receptor binding
        ↓                                        ↓
   Caspase 9 activation                 Caspase 8 activation
              ↘                        ↙
                Caspase 3 activation
                        ↓
                    Apoptosis
   ```

   Apoptosis is deregulated in many tumours, resulting in uncontrolled cell division despite the presence of significant DNA damage. One strategy for the discovery of new anti-cancer drugs has been to examine traditional medicinal herbs.

   A study was carried out to investigate the effect of an extract of the wild ginger plant, *Asiasari radix*, on the initiation of apoptosis in colon cancer cells.

   Colon cancer cells were treated with this extract and then assessed for the presence of apoptotic cells. The percentage increase in cells undergoing apoptosis was calculated by comparing the level of apoptosis in treated cells with that in untreated controls as shown in Figure 2.

   Figure 2

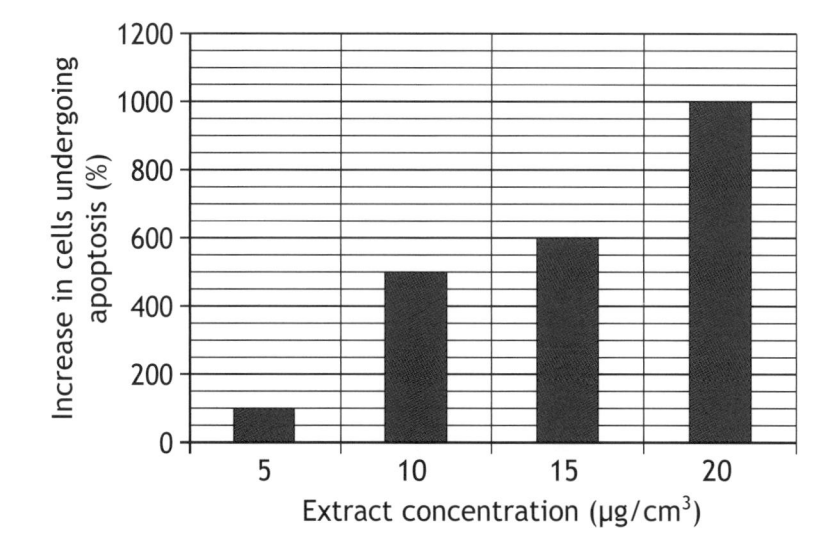

   Bar chart showing Increase in cells undergoing apoptosis (%) against Extract concentration (μg/cm³):
   - 5 μg/cm³: 100%
   - 10 μg/cm³: 500%
   - 15 μg/cm³: 600%
   - 20 μg/cm³: 1000%

1. **(continued)**

   To investigate the involvement of caspases in this process of apoptosis, the experiment was repeated using a single dose of extract (10 μg/cm^3) but with the addition of a variety of caspase inhibitors (drugs known to prevent the activation of one or more caspases). Inhibitors used included an inhibitor known to prevent activation of all caspases (all ci) and individual inhibitors of caspase 3 (ci 3), caspase 8 (ci 8) and caspase 9 (ci 9). Percentage changes in the number of cells undergoing apoptosis compared to untreated cancer cells are shown in Figure 3.

   Figure 3

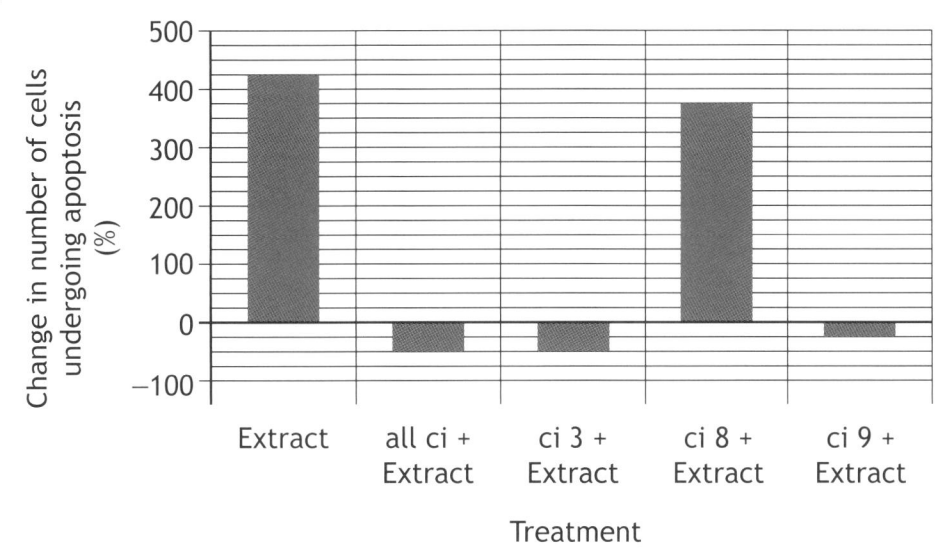

   The distribution of the cancer cells across the different phases of the cell cycle was then investigated by measuring the DNA content of the cells. Cultures of cells were treated with 10 μg/cm^3 extract or left untreated for 24 hours as a control and then the DNA content of 10,000 cells was analysed for each cell culture. Results for treated cells are shown in Figure 4A and for control cells in Figure 4B. DNA content is displayed with arbitrary units where 200 units represents the DNA content of a non-dividing diploid cell.

   Figure 4A   **Figure 4B**

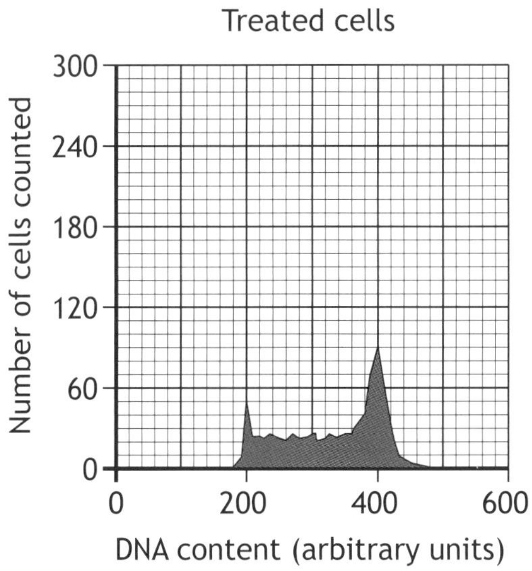

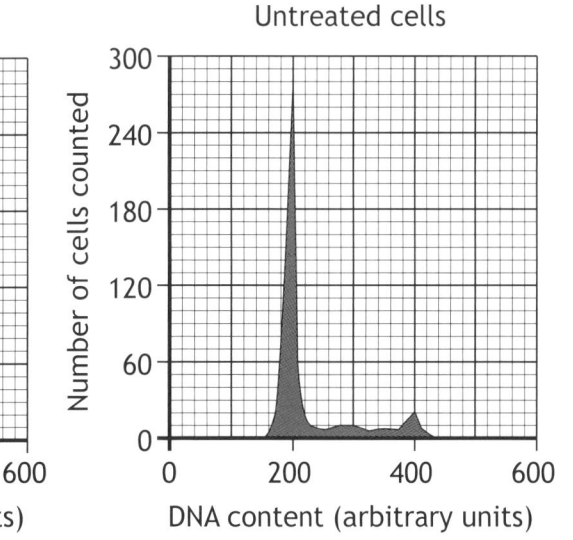

ADVANCED HIGHER

2018

National Qualifications 2018

X707/77/02

Biology
Section 1 — Questions

TUESDAY, 15 MAY
9:00 AM – 11:30 AM

Instructions for the completion of Section 1 are given on *Page two* of your question and answer booklet X707/77/01.

Record your answers on the answer grid on *Page three* of your question and answer booklet.

Before leaving the examination room you must give your question and answer booklet to the Invigilator; if you do not, you may lose all the marks for this paper.

SECTION 1 — 25 marks

Attempt ALL questions

1. Which row in the table describes properties of proteins that allow them to be separated using the techniques shown?

| | Protein separation technique ||
	Centrifugation	Gel electrophoresis
A	density	charge
B	charge	density
C	shape	charge
D	charge	shape

2. Which of the pairs of cell types are fused in order to produce monoclonal antibodies?

   A T lymphocyte and myeloma

   B B lymphocyte and myeloma

   C T lymphocyte and hybridoma

   D B lymphocyte and hybridoma

3. The three-dimensional structure of a protein is shown.

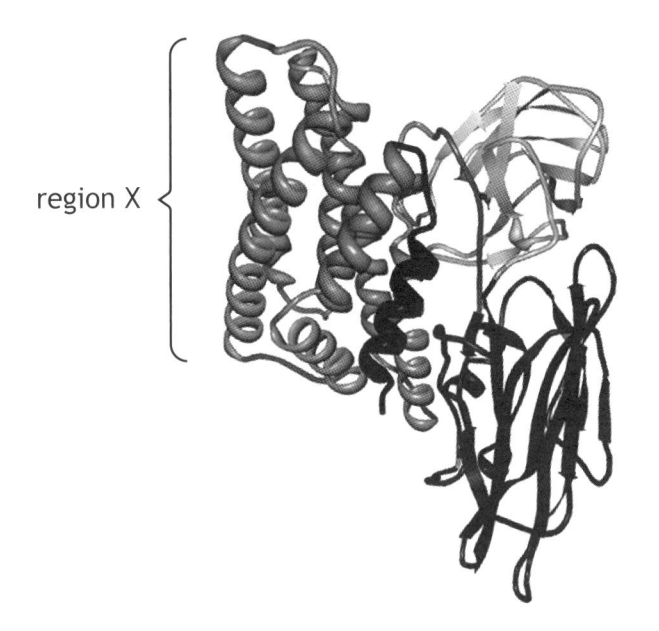

region X

Which row in the table describes region X?

	Type of secondary structure	Bonding that stabilises secondary structure
A	β-sheet	peptide
B	α-helix	peptide
C	β-sheet	hydrogen
D	α-helix	hydrogen

[Turn over

4. The diagram shows some interactions between amino acid R-groups in a polypeptide chain.

Which letter shows hydrophobic interactions?

5. A student is preparing media for an experiment to investigate the effect of an inhibitor on cell growth. Flask 1 contains a control medium with no inhibitor.

The concentration of the stock inhibitor solution used to prepare the final solution is **80%**.

Flask	Inhibitor volume (cm³)	Glucose volume (cm³)	FBS volume (cm³)	Buffer volume (cm³)	Final inhibitor concentration (%)
1	0·00	1·00	5·00	19·00	0
2		1·00	5·00		20

What volumes of inhibitor and buffer should be added to flask 2 to give 25 cm³ of medium with an inhibitor concentration of 20%?

A 4·75 cm³ inhibitor + 20·25 cm³ buffer

B 4·75 cm³ inhibitor + 14·25 cm³ buffer

C 6·25 cm³ inhibitor + 18·75 cm³ buffer

D 6·25 cm³ inhibitor + 12·75 cm³ buffer

6. Transcription of gene Z only occurs when its transcription factor is dephosphorylated.

The distribution of the transcription factor together with the activities of a protein kinase and protein phosphatase specific to this transcription factor are shown in the table.

Tissue	Transcription factor present	Protein kinase activity	Protein phosphatase activity
Muscle	−	−	+
Heart	+	+	−
Brain	+	−	+

Gene Z is transcribed in the

A brain only

B heart only

C muscle and brain only

D heart and brain only.

7. The effect of changing the concentration of extracellular potassium ions on the function of sodium potassium pumps was investigated.

Starting with an extracellular solution containing no potassium ions, as the concentration of potassium ions is increased the pumps would be expected to

A pump out potassium ions at a faster rate

B stay in their phosphorylated conformation for longer

C pump in sodium ions at a faster rate

D hydrolyse ATP at a faster rate.

[Turn over

8. A sample of 10⁶ cells was found to contain 0·4 mg protein. Actin comprises 4·5% of the total protein. 42 g of actin contains $6·02 \times 10^{20}$ molecules.

   1 g = 1000 mg

   The number of actin molecules **per cell** is

   A $2·58 \times 10^8$
   B $2·58 \times 10^{10}$
   C $2·58 \times 10^{11}$
   D $2·58 \times 10^{14}$

9. An outcome of the activation of a cell's thyroid hormone receptors by thyroxine is

   A   decreased production of Na/KATPase
   B   increased production of Na/KATPase
   C   decreased metabolic rate
   D   opening of ligand-gated ion channels.

10. The flow diagram shows part of the ADH signal transduction pathway in a collecting duct cell.

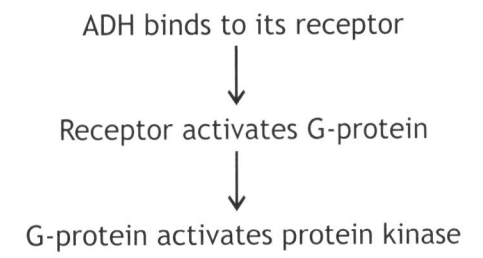

ADH binds to its receptor
↓
Receptor activates G-protein
↓
G-protein activates protein kinase

Which row in the table shows how this pathway would be altered in an individual with diabetes insipidus?

	Concentration of inactive G-proteins	Phosphorylation of proteins
A	decreased	decreased
B	decreased	increased
C	increased	decreased
D	increased	increased

11. Which row in the table describes the states of the proteins p53 and Rb that would increase the rate of cell division?

	Protein	
	p53	Rb
A	activated	phosphorylated
B	inhibited	phosphorylated
C	activated	dephosphorylated
D	inhibited	dephosphorylated

[Turn over

12. Which diagram shows the correct positions of the cell cycle checkpoints?

    Checkpoint is represented by |

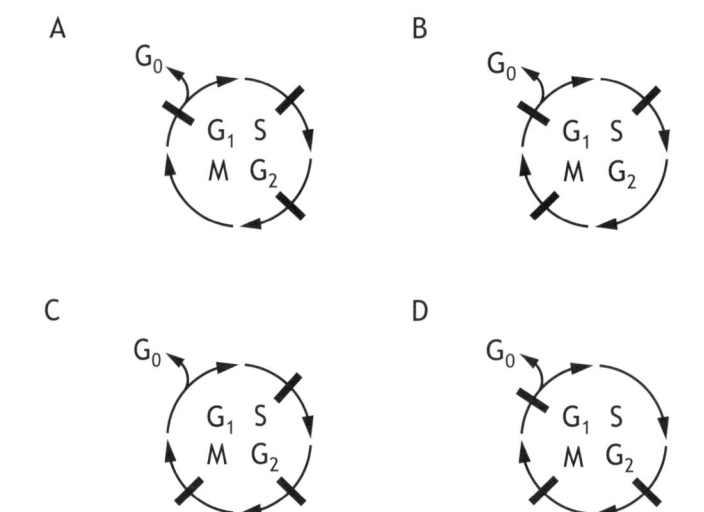

13. In a study of transmission of the rabies virus by vampire bats, the density of bat colonies was estimated using mark and recapture techniques.

    The total population estimate is given by (MC)/R where the first sample captured is M, the second sample captured is C and the number recaptured is R.

    One colony was estimated to have a bat population of 440 following the capture of a second sample of 64 bats, of which 8 were marked.

    The number of bats captured initially, marked and released was

    A 32
    B 55
    C 110
    D 128

14. Which of the following describes the purpose of a randomised block design?

    A Controlling for confounding variables
    B Ranking sample data
    C Ensuring that sampling is representative
    D Monitoring the dependent variable

15. Merlins are small birds of prey which chase and capture skylarks. The effect of skylark song on hunting by merlins was studied.

Graph 1 shows the number of successful and unsuccessful attacks on skylarks showing different singing behaviours.

Graph 2 shows how the different singing behaviours affected the mean duration of chases by merlins attacking skylarks.

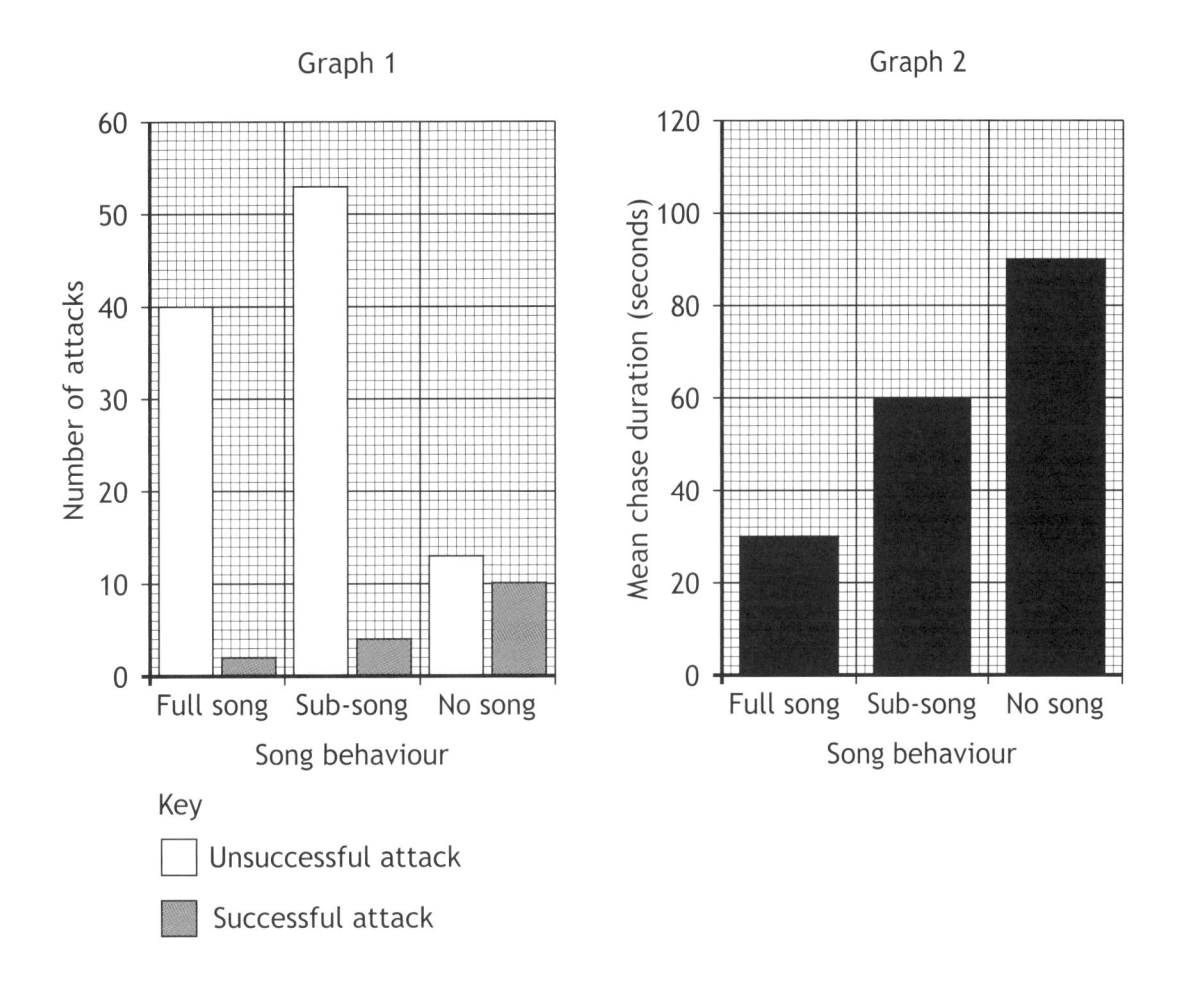

Which of the following generalisations about skylark singing behaviour is valid?

A No song decreases the number of attacks by merlins and the time they will chase.

B No song increases the success of attacks by merlins and the time they will chase.

C No song increases the number of attacks by merlins and the time they will chase.

D No song decreases the success of attacks by merlins and the time they will chase.

[Turn over

16. Humans and many other primates have opposable thumbs. In the giant panda, a modified wrist bone forms a false 'thumb' which is used along with the five digits to manipulate bamboo.

    The list shows processes related to evolution.

    1   Convergent evolution
    2   Divergent evolution
    3   Natural selection

    Evolution of the thumbs of primates and the false 'thumbs' of giant pandas has involved

    A   1 only
    B   2 only
    C   1 and 3 only
    D   2 and 3 only.

17. Which statement includes representatives of all three domains of life?

    A   Insects can be vectors for bacterial infections in plants.
    B   Photoreceptor proteins are found in archaea, plants and animals.
    C   Scientists have cloned genes from archaea that can be expressed in *Escherichia coli*.
    D   Diseases in potato crops can be caused by the transmission of viruses by nematodes.

18. Haemophilia A is a sex-linked condition that slows blood clotting. The allele for normal clotting (X^H) is dominant to the allele for haemophilia A (X^h).

The diagram gives information about the inheritance of haemophilia A in one family.

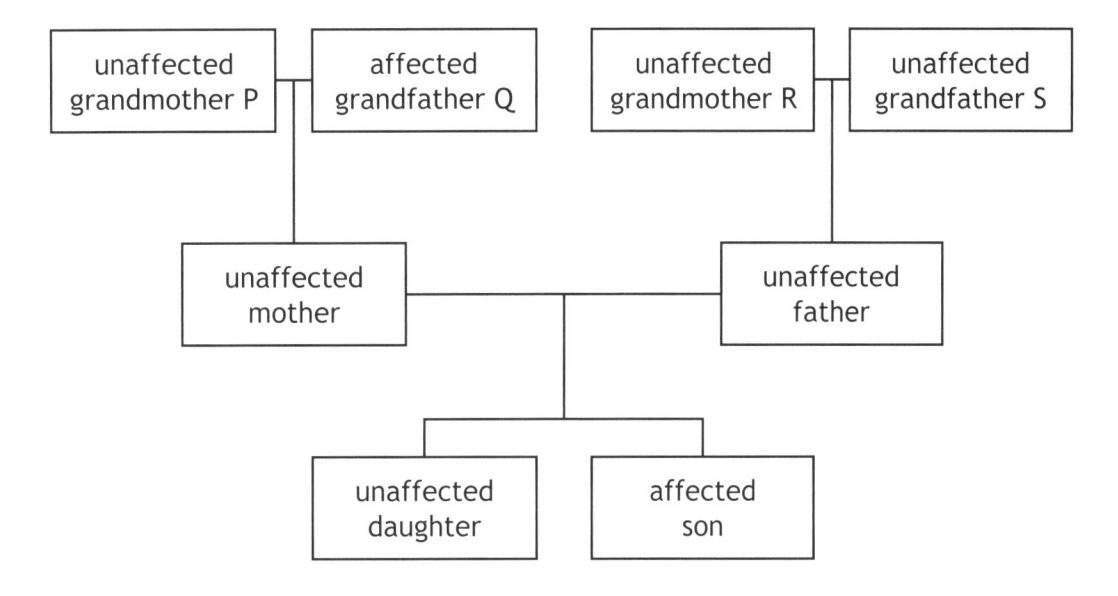

```
[unaffected grandmother P]—[affected grandfather Q]    [unaffected grandmother R]—[unaffected grandfather S]
                    │                                              │
              [unaffected mother]—————————————————[unaffected father]
                                        │
                        ┌───────────────┴───────────────┐
                 [unaffected daughter]           [affected son]
```

From the information given, which of the statements is true?

A The genotype of grandmother P must be $X^H X^h$ but the genotype of grandmother R cannot be determined.

B The genotype of neither grandmother can be determined.

C The genotype of both the unaffected mother and her daughter must be $X^H X^h$.

D The genotype of neither the mother or her daughter can be determined.

[Turn over

19. Red deer in Scotland have no natural predators. Control of the growth of a population to prevent it from outstripping resources is achieved by annual culling. The number killed annually must be greater than the *recruitment* (annual population increase due to births). Since birth rates vary, computer models are used to generate three estimates for recruitment based on birth rates of 30%, 35% and 40%. The number of red deer culled annually is recorded in different areas.

The table shows cull totals for one year in four areas, along with estimated recruitment at each birth rate.

Area	Cull total	Estimated recruitment based on birth rate		
		30%	35%	40%
North Ross	2654	2151	2557	2963
East Loch Ericht	887	897	1066	1234
Breadalbane	3026	1396	1659	1922
Knoydart	1082	1079	1283	1487

If the true birth rate is 35%, the area(s) in which the cull is sufficient to prevent population growth would be

A North Ross, East Loch Ericht, Breadalbane and Knoydart

B North Ross, Breadalbane and Knoydart only

C North Ross and Breadalbane only

D Breadalbane only.

20. Many species display some characteristics that are typical of r-selection and some that are typical of K-selection.

   Which of the following species displays **only** K-selected characteristics?

   A Leatherback turtles: lay up to nine large clutches of eggs per breeding season; hatchlings receive no parental care; small proportion survives to reach sexual maturity.

   B Arctic terns: usually lay two eggs per clutch; adults are aggressive in defence of their young; more than 50% of offspring live to 30 years of age.

   C English oak trees: slow-growing; do not produce seeds until at least 40 years of age; mature trees produce many thousands of seeds annually but only a small proportion germinate.

   D Common dandelions: readily colonise disturbed ground; grow rapidly; flower several times a year; produce many seeds per flower head.

21. During the ritualised courtship in peafowl, *Pavo muticus*, the male spreads and shakes his tail feathers to attract a female before stepping back and bowing. This is followed by loud mating calls.

   This type of fixed action pattern response can be a result of

   A honest signals
   B imprinting
   C male-male rivalry
   D species-specific sign stimuli.

22. An *in vivo* study involves observations made in

   A the natural habitat of an animal
   B a living cell culture in the laboratory
   C a living organism
   D extracts prepared from living tissues.

[Turn over

23. Eggs of the parasitic liver fluke *Leucochloridium paradoxum* are found on vegetation and can be eaten by marsh snails, *Succinea putris*. Inside snails, eggs develop into larvae which move to the ends of their tentacles. The tentacles become swollen and brightly coloured, resembling striped caterpillars. Infected snails become more active during daylight when predatory birds mistake the abnormal tentacles for caterpillars and eat them. The larvae within the tentacles complete their life cycle within the birds' bodies. Eggs are passed out of the birds in faeces.

Which items on the list represent part of the extended phenotype of the parasite?

1 Prey selection by birds
2 Modification of snail tentacles
3 Changed activity of snails
4 Feeding method of snails

A 1 and 2 only
B 1 and 3 only
C 2 and 3 only
D 3 and 4 only

24. Which row in the table identifies white blood cells capable of long term survival as a part of immunological memory in mammals?

	Type of white blood cell			
	B lymphocytes	T lymphocytes	Phagocytes	Natural killers
A		✓		✓
B	✓		✓	
C			✓	✓
D	✓	✓		

25. The graphs show data derived from a study investigating the effectiveness of the drug praziquantel (PZQ) on Ugandan children with symptoms of schistosomiasis.

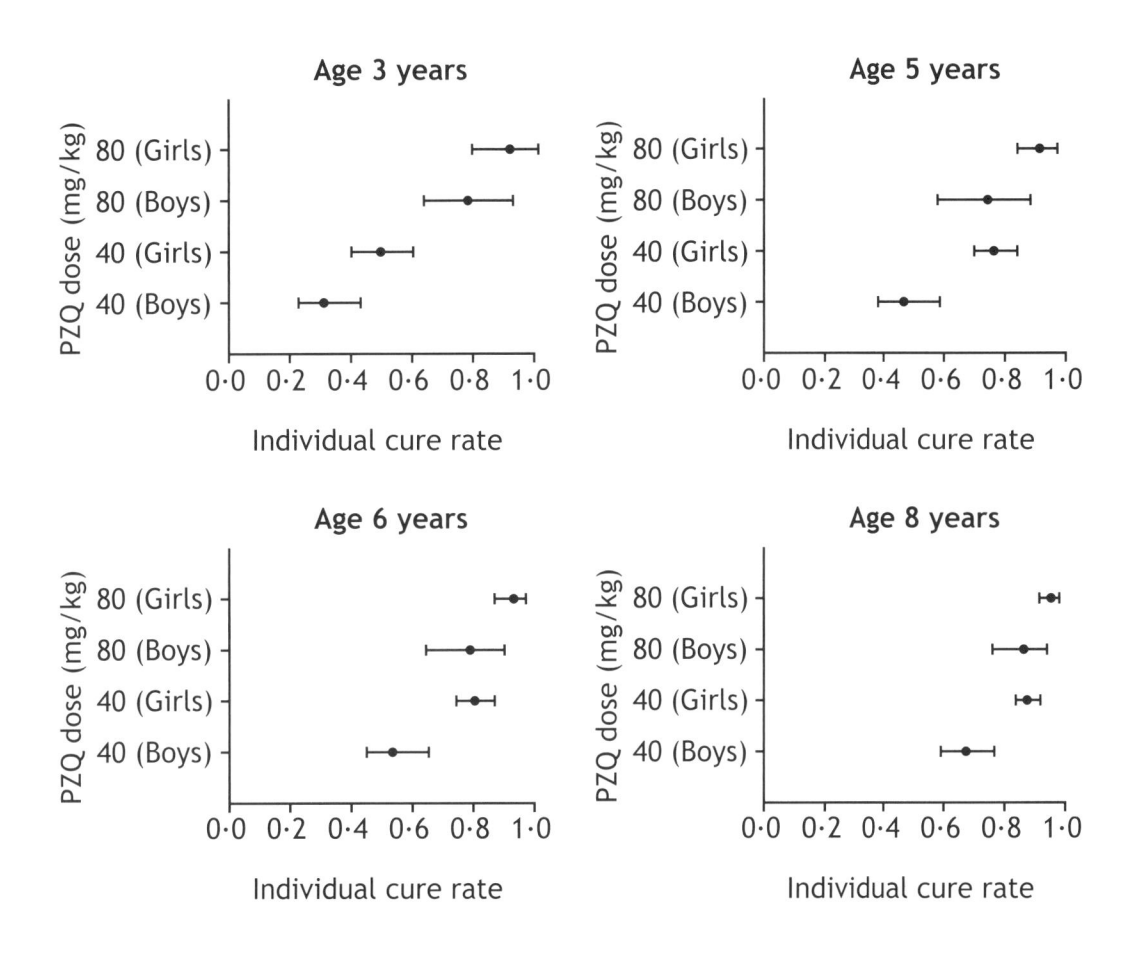

At what age does the data suggest that children would receive most benefit by increasing the dose of the drug?

A 3 years

B 5 years

C 6 years

D 8 years

[END OF SECTION 1. NOW ATTEMPT THE QUESTIONS IN SECTION 2 OF YOUR QUESTION AND ANSWER BOOKLET]

FOR OFFICIAL USE

National Qualifications 2018

Mark

X707/77/01

**Biology
Section 1 — Answer Grid
and Section 2**

TUESDAY, 15 MAY
9:00 AM – 11:30 AM

Fill in these boxes and read what is printed below.

Full name of centre

Town

Forename(s)

Surname

Number of seat

Date of birth
Day   Month   Year

Scottish candidate number

Total marks — 90

SECTION 1 — 25 marks

Attempt ALL questions.

Instructions for the completion of Section 1 are given on *Page two*.

SECTION 2 — 65 marks

Attempt ALL questions.

A supplementary sheet for question 1 is enclosed inside the front cover of this question paper.

Write your answers clearly in the spaces provided in this booklet. Additional space for answers and rough work is provided at the end of this booklet. If you use this space you must clearly identify the question number you are attempting. Any rough work must be written in this booklet. Score through your rough work when you have written your final copy.

Use **blue** or **black** ink.

Before leaving the examination room you must give this booklet to the Invigilator; if you do not, you may lose all the marks for this paper.

SQA

SECTION 1 — 25 marks

The questions for Section 1 are contained in the question paper X707/77/02.

Read these and record your answers on the answer grid on *Page three* opposite.

Use **blue** or **black** ink. Do NOT use gel pens or pencil.

1. The answer to each question is **either** A, B, C or D. Decide what your answer is, then fill in the appropriate bubble (see sample question below).

2. There is **only one correct** answer to each question.

3. Any rough working should be done on the additional space for answers and rough work at the end of this booklet.

Sample question

The thigh bone is called the

    A   humerus

    B   femur

    C   tibia

    D   fibula.

The correct answer is **B** — femur. The answer **B** bubble has been clearly filled in (see below).

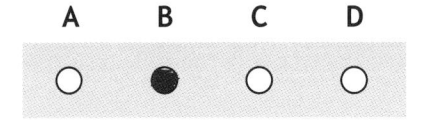

Changing an answer

If you decide to change your answer, cancel your first answer by putting a cross through it (see below) and fill in the answer you want. The answer below has been changed to **D**.

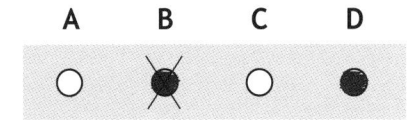

If you then decide to change back to an answer you have already scored out, put a tick (✓) to the **right** of the answer you want, as shown below:

SECTION 1 — Answer Grid

	A	B	C	D
1	○	○	○	○
2	○	○	○	○
3	○	○	○	○
4	○	○	○	○
5	○	○	○	○
6	○	○	○	○
7	○	○	○	○
8	○	○	○	○
9	○	○	○	○
10	○	○	○	○
11	○	○	○	○
12	○	○	○	○
13	○	○	○	○
14	○	○	○	○
15	○	○	○	○
16	○	○	○	○
17	○	○	○	○
18	○	○	○	○
19	○	○	○	○
20	○	○	○	○
21	○	○	○	○
22	○	○	○	○
23	○	○	○	○
24	○	○	○	○
25	○	○	○	○

[Turn over

SECTION 2 — 65 marks

Attempt ALL questions

Question 11 contains a choice

1. Read through the supplementary sheet for question 1 before attempting this question.

    (a) Explain why the rate of uptake by GLUT transporters levels off at high glucose concentrations.

    (b) **Refer to Figure 2 in the supplementary sheet for question 1.**

    Figure 2 shows GLUT3 has the lowest K_M for glucose.

    Explain how this supports the conclusion that GLUT3 has the highest affinity for glucose.

    (c) The rate of glucose transport at a given glucose concentration can be calculated using the formula:

    $$V = \frac{V_{max} \times [G]}{K_M + [G]}$$

    V = rate of glucose transport

    $[G]$ = glucose concentration (mmol per litre)

    GLUT2 transporters, found mainly in liver and pancreatic cells, have a K_M of 17 mmol per litre. At this concentration of glucose the rate of transport by GLUT2 is 0·02 mmol/min.

    The physiological range of blood glucose concentration in a healthy individual after fasting ranges from approximately 3·9 to 5·5 mmol per litre.

    (i) Calculate the rate of glucose transport by GLUT2 when the blood glucose concentration is 5·5 mmol per litre.

    Space for calculation

    _____ mmol/min

1. (c) (continued)

   (ii) Increases in blood glucose concentration lead to increased insulin production by the pancreas. Glucose uptake by GLUT2 is important for this response because as glucose entry via GLUT2 increases the pancreas synthesises more insulin.

   Suggest why the high K_M of GLUT2 is important in this mechanism for sensing glucose concentration. **1**

   (d) Release of insulin into the bloodstream leads to a rapid increase in the transport of glucose into muscle and fat cells via GLUT4.

   Explain why this normal response to insulin does not happen in individuals with type 2 diabetes. **2**

   (e) **Refer to Figure 3 in the supplementary sheet for question 1.**

   Describe the trend shown in Figure 3. **1**

   (f) Blood serum caffeine levels in people who regularly consume caffeine are typically around 6 μmol per litre.

   Using Figure 3 predict, with justification, whether this level of caffeine consumption would be likely to have a large effect on the transport of glucose by GLUT1. **1**

   [Turn over

2. (a) The figure represents the four subunits (two α, two β) of a haemoglobin molecule before and after binding with oxygen molecules.

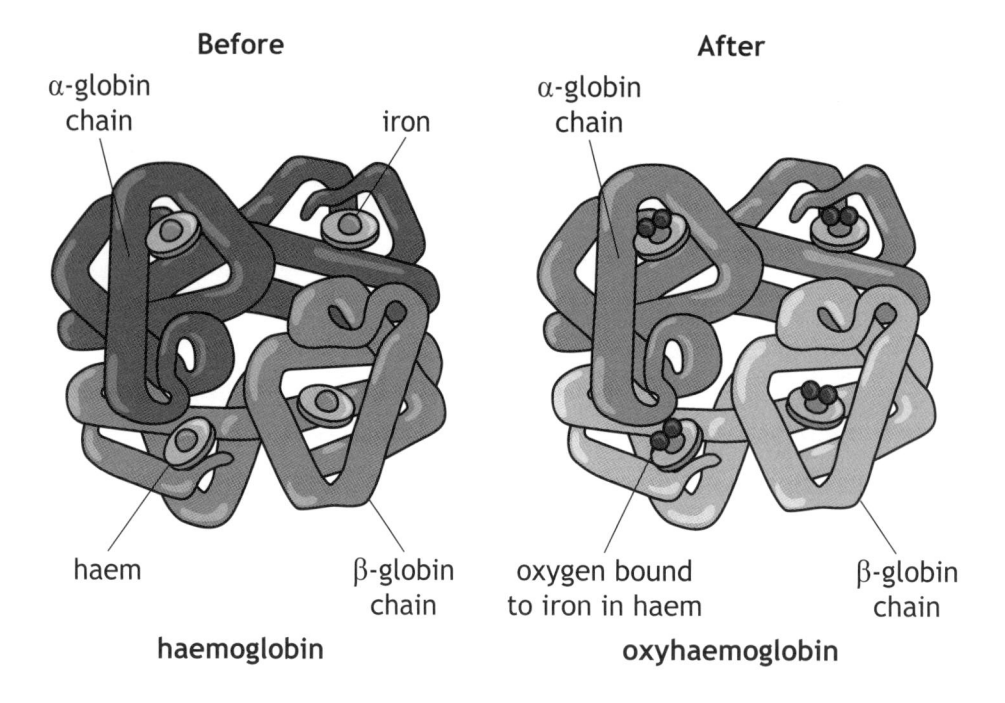

Before
α-globin chain
iron
haem
β-globin chain
haemoglobin

After
α-globin chain
oxygen bound to iron in haem
β-globin chain
oxyhaemoglobin

(i) Name the process whereby binding of oxygen to one subunit of haemoglobin alters the affinity of the remaining subunits.

(ii) Tissues with higher metabolic rates require more oxygen. These tissues produce more carbon dioxide, which dissolves in tissue fluids to form carbonic acid.

Explain how this increases oxygen delivery at these tissues.

(iii) Haem is a non-protein component important in the function of haemoglobin.

State the term used to describe such a component.

2. (continued)

(b) During one stage in its life cycle, the human parasite *Plasmodium* enters a red blood cell. In order to obtain amino acids that it requires, it digests haemoglobin using a mixture of protease enzymes. This releases the product haem, which is toxic to the parasite. Haem is then converted into non-toxic haemozoin by another enzyme called HDP.

```
                 Stage 1              Stage 2
              Proteases              HDP
Haemoglobin  ─────────→    Haem    ─────────→   Haemozoin
                         (toxic)                (non-toxic)
```

(i) Name the human disease caused by *Plasmodium*. **1**

(ii) Chloroquine is one of a number of drugs used to treat this disease.

Suggest how drugs such as chloroquine, that target Stage 2, may provide an effective treatment. **2**

[Turn over

3. The diagram shows stages in the transmission of a nerve impulse.

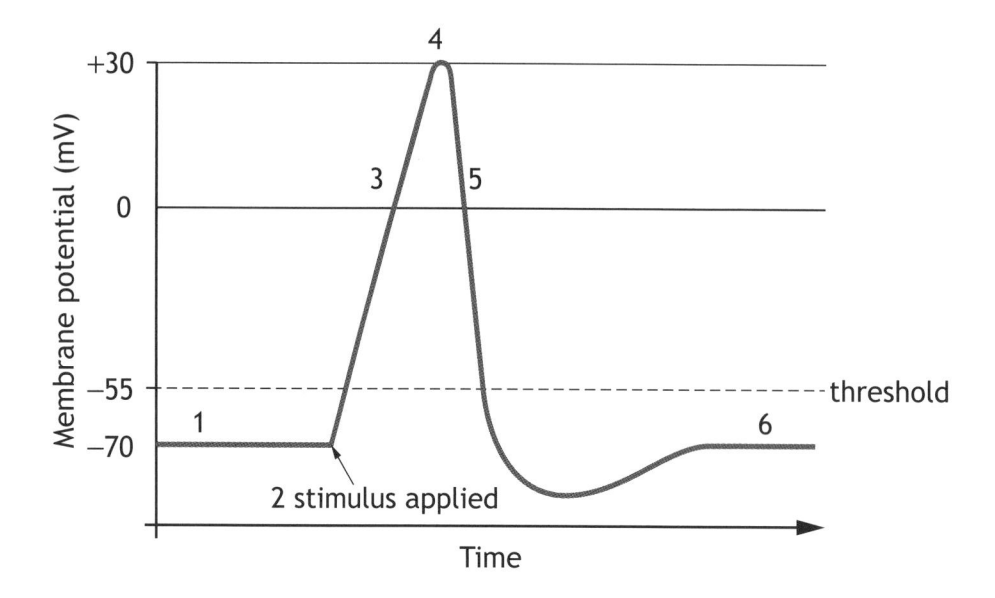

1. Membrane potential before nerve impulse initiated
2. Binding of a neurotransmitter to a ligand-gated sodium ion (Na$^+$) channel
3. Voltage gated Na$^+$ channels open
4. Voltage gated Na$^+$ channels become inactivated
5. Voltage gated potassium ion (K$^+$) channels open
6. Membrane potential after nerve impulse has passed

(a) (i) State the term that describes the membrane potential at points 1 and 6. **1**

(ii) Use the diagram to calculate the change in membrane potential between points 1 and 4. **1**

Space for calculation

3. (a) (continued)

   (iii) Use the information in the diagram to explain the importance of K$^+$ channels in nerve transmission. **2**

   (b) Tetrodotoxin is a poison found in some fish, such as the pufferfish, which has its effect at stage three of the process shown in the diagram.

   Suggest a possible mechanism for the toxicity of this substance. **1**

[Turn over

4. The neurotransmitter gamma-aminobutyric acid (GABA) binds to GABA$_A$ receptors in nerve cells. GABA$_A$ receptors are a family of structurally related transmembrane ion channels. One proposed structure of a GABA$_A$ receptor is shown in the diagram.

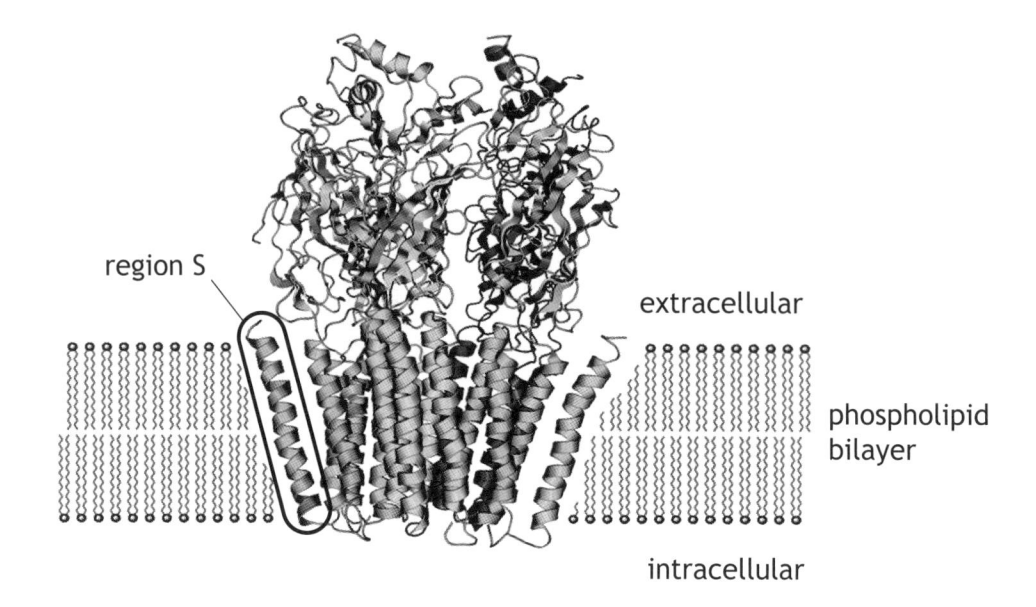

(a) (i) All GABA$_A$ receptors consist of five subunits.

Name the level of protein structure describing several connected polypeptide subunits. 1

_____

(ii) Region S has some of the R groups in contact with the bilayer.

Predict the class of R groups to which these amino acids belong. 1

_____

4. (continued)

(b) It has been suggested that different forms of the GABA$_A$ receptor subunit can arise as a result of alternative RNA splicing.

Explain how alternative RNA splicing could result in the production of variant forms of GABA$_A$ receptor subunits. **2**

(c) Suggest what happens to the receptor protein when GABA binds to it. **1**

(d) The drug diazepam increases the effect of GABA molecules by binding to a secondary (allosteric) binding site on GABA$_A$ receptors.

State the term used to describe the effect of diazepam on GABA$_A$ receptors. **1**

[Turn over

5. Microtubules are found in all eukaryotic cells.

(a) Name the globular protein of which microtubules are composed.

(b) Name the structure from which microtubules radiate.

(c) The formation and functioning of mitotic spindle fibres depends on the action of specific enzymes such as *cytoplasmic dynein*.

The role of cytoplasmic dynein in mitosis was investigated. Preparations of purified antibodies that inhibit cytoplasmic dynein's action were injected into cultured mammalian cells at different stages in mitosis. Comparable cells were injected with a buffer solution containing no antibodies.

The figure shows a cell undergoing microinjection.

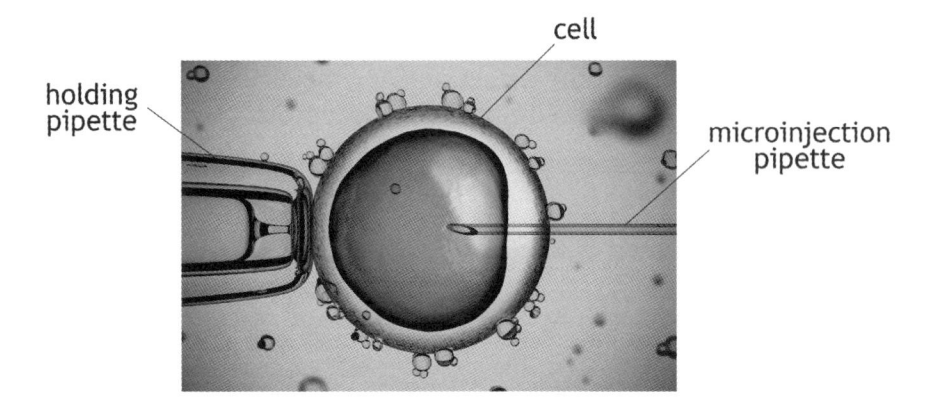

The following results were obtained.
- Mitosis was blocked in 73% of the cells injected with the antibody at 12 mg/cm³ during prophase.
- Injection of buffer alone had no effect on mitosis.
- Lower concentrations of antibodies (6 mg/cm³) had no obvious effect on mitosis.
- Cells injected with antibody during metaphase or anaphase completed mitosis with no detectable differences compared to cells injected with buffer alone.

5. (c) (continued)

   (i) State the purpose of injecting cells with buffer solution only. **1**

   (ii) Give a valid conclusion for this experiment. **1**

(d) Once mitosis is complete, the cytoplasm separates to give two daughter cells.

   State the term used to describe this process. **1**

[Turn over

6. The following customer comment was used to promote a product intended to treat cats that suffered from cancer.

'My cat was diagnosed with bone cancer three years ago. Her leg was amputated, and I was told that she would only live for another six months. I saw advertising for *Vivafel* and immediately started her on this product. She has been in remission and healthy ever since. I thoroughly recommend this product and the effect it has on cancer in cats.'

(a) (i) What is the conclusion that appears to have been drawn by the cat's owner?

(ii) Apart from being based on one cat, give **one** reason why this conclusion is invalid.

(b) Suggest why the results of the treatment are unlikely to be caused by a placebo effect, in which even a dummy treatment can bring about some improvement.

6. (continued)

   (c) Trials to test the effectiveness of the drug Vivafel were set up using living cats.

   (i) Describe **one** way to ensure that these trials were ethical. 1

   (ii) State an appropriate null hypothesis for these trials. 1

[Turn over

7. Where it is impractical to measure every individual in a population, a representative sample of the population must be obtained.

Discuss the principles and strategies that should be employed in the collection of representative samples. **4**

[Turn over for next question

DO NOT WRITE ON THIS PAGE

8. Giraffes are the tallest terrestrial animals, growing up to 5 m tall. Approximately half of a giraffe's height is due to its long neck. Modern giraffes have evolved from ancestors with much shorter necks.

The figures represent two different hypotheses regarding the evolution of the giraffe's long neck.

Competing browsers hypothesis   Necks for sex hypothesis

Charles Darwin suggested that the long necks evolved by natural selection: longer necks allowed animals to feed higher up trees with less competition — the 'competing browsers' hypothesis.

This hypothesis was not thought to be consistent with all the evidence available and a rival hypothesis, 'necks for sex', has been put forward. This suggests long necks have evolved as a result of sexual selection through male–male rivalry, where male giraffes fight for access to females by standing side by side and hitting each other with their heads.

(a) Use the competing browsers hypothesis to explain how long necks evolved by natural selection.

2

8. (continued)

(b) Long necks evolved around 13 million years ago when much of the African forest was replaced by grassland with a greatly reduced number of trees.

Explain how this supports the competing browsers hypothesis. **1**

(c) (i) Explain how long necks could have evolved through sexual selection. **1**

(ii) A study published in 2013 concluded that there was no sexual dimorphism in neck length in giraffes.

Suggest how this finding would cast doubt on the necks for sex hypothesis. **1**

[Turn over

9. New Zealand mud snails, *Potamopyrgus antipodarum,* are widely distributed in freshwater streams and lakes in New Zealand. Snail populations consist of females that reproduce asexually by parthenogenesis together with females that reproduce sexually by cross fertilisation with males.

(a) State **two** disadvantages of sexual reproduction.

1 _____

2 _____

(b) New Zealand mud snails are commonly infected with parasitic worms of the genus *Microphallus*. Sexual reproduction is more common in the snails when the prevalence of parasites is high.

Explain how this observation supports the Red Queen hypothesis.

(c) The New Zealand mud snail has become invasive by spreading beyond its native habitat to colonise areas of Europe and North America.

Suggest why invasive populations are found to be composed entirely of parthenogenic females.

[Turn over for next question

DO NOT WRITE ON THIS PAGE

10. The figure shows an Ebola virus, cause of Ebola virus disease (EVD), prevalent in a number of West and Central African countries. The virus is transmitted to people from wild animals and outbreaks may then occur through human to human transmission.

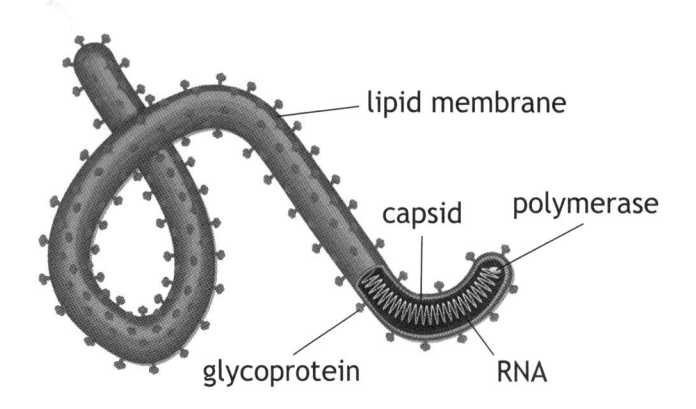

(a) Ebola viruses have a diameter of 8×10^{-2} μm.

Give this measurement in nanometres (nm). (1 nm = 10^{-3} μm) 1

Space for calculation

(b) The flow diagram shows some stages in the replication of this virus.

Virus attaches to host cell receptors
↓
Virus enters host cell
↓
Viral RNA is used as a template to synthesise complementary mRNA
↓
mRNA is translated into viral proteins
↓
Viral RNA replicated
↓
New virus particles assembled
↓
Viruses released and cell destroyed

Explain why the Ebola virus **cannot** be regarded as a retrovirus. 1

10. (continued)

   (c) EVD symptoms result from viral disruption of immune cell function such as the loss of lymphocytes by apoptosis.

   State the cause of cell death during apoptosis.

   (d) The genes coding for some Ebola virus proteins have a high rate of mutation.

   Why would this make development of a vaccine more difficult?

   (e) EVD has a very high mortality rate. Some researchers have suggested that new treatments should not be assessed by clinical trials that use negative control groups.

   State whether you agree or disagree with this suggestion.

   Justify your answer.

   (f) Apart from medical treatments, suggest **one** measure that could be effective in controlling or preventing outbreaks of EVD in the tropical regions of Africa.

   [Turn over for next question

11. Answer **either A or B** in the space below and on *Page twenty-five*.

   A   Discuss the concept of niche under the following headings:

   (i) realised and fundamental niche;   3

   (ii) features of parasite niches.   6

   OR

   B   Discuss the formation of variable gametes during meiosis under the following headings:

   (i) the activity of homologous chromosomes;   7

   (ii) meiosis II.   2

SPACE FOR ANSWER FOR QUESTION 11

[END OF QUESTION PAPER]

ADDITIONAL SPACE FOR ANSWERS AND ROUGH WORK

AH

National
Qualifications
2018

X707/77/11

**Biology
Supplementary Sheet**

TUESDAY, 15 MAY
9:00 AM – 11:30 AM

Supplementary sheet for question 1

1. The diffusion of glucose across the plasma membrane of mammalian cells is facilitated by a family of related proteins called GLUT transporters. GLUT transporters have a specific binding site for glucose which alternately faces inside and outside the cell. The orientation of the binding site is brought about by a change in conformation as shown in Figure 1.

Figure 1

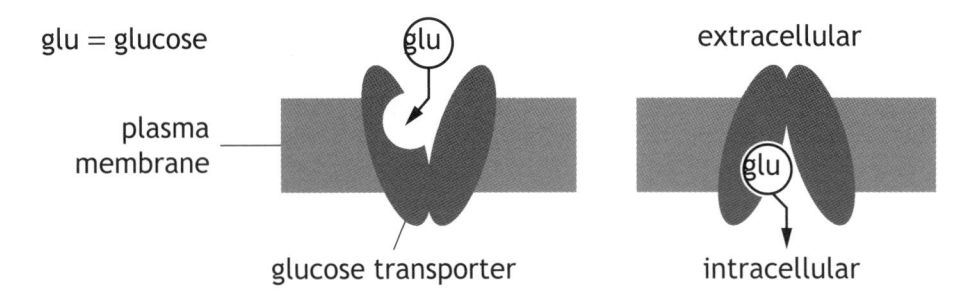

glu = glucose

plasma membrane

glucose transporter

extracellular

intracellular

Several studies have measured the changes in rates of glucose uptake by GLUT transporters as the concentration of glucose is increased.

Results for four different GLUT transporters are shown in Figure 2.

For each type of GLUT transporter, the rate of transport levels off to a maximum value that is termed V_{max}. The glucose concentration at which the rate of transport is **half** V_{max} is defined as the K_M of the transporter. K_M values for four types of GLUT are shown in Figure 2.

Figure 2

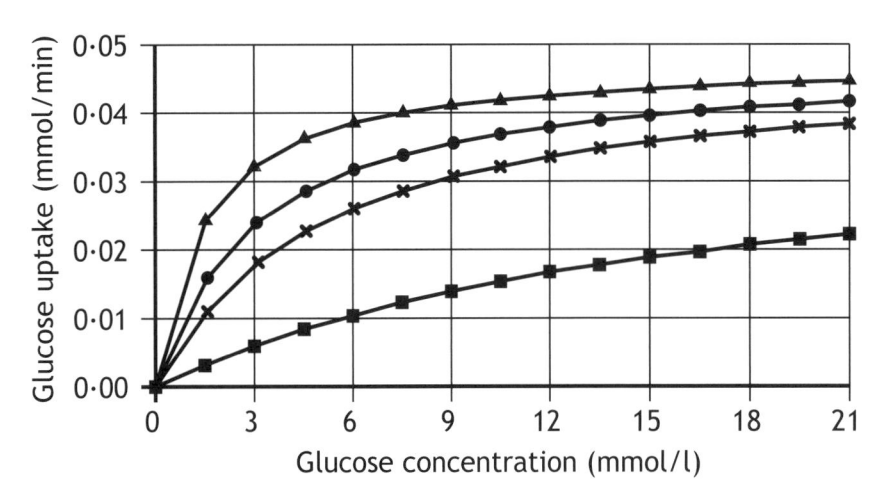

Glucose uptake (mmol/min) vs Glucose concentration (mmol/l)

Key

▲—▲ GLUT3 (K_M = 1·4 mmol/l)   ●—● GLUT1 (K_M = 3·0 mmol/l)

✗—✗ GLUT4 (K_M = 5·0 mmol/l)   ■—■ GLUT2 (K_M = 17·0 mmol/l)

1. (continued)

Studies have suggested that the chemical caffeine is an inhibitor of glucose transport by GLUT1.

Figure 3 shows data obtained from a recent study of the effect of increasing caffeine concentration on the uptake of glucose by GLUT1. The uptake of glucose in these experiments was measured per litre of intracellular fluid.

Figure 3

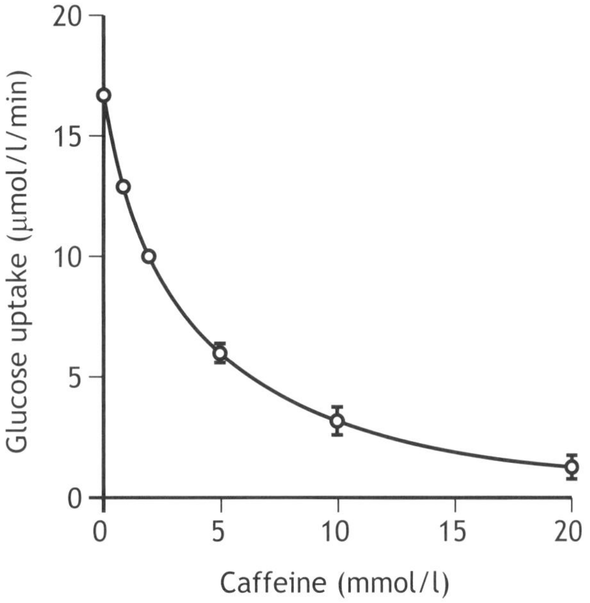

[END OF SUPPLEMENTARY SHEET]

ADVANCED HIGHER

Answers

ANSWERS FOR SQA ADVANCED HIGHER BIOLOGY 2018

ADVANCED HIGHER BIOLOGY 2016

Section 1

Question	Answer	Max mark
1.	D	1
2.	A	1
3.	A	1
4.	B	1
5.	C	1
6.	B	1
7.	B	1
8.	C	1
9.	C	1
10.	D	1
11.	B	1
12.	A	1
13.	B	1

Question	Answer	Max mark
14.	A	1
15.	B	1
16.	D	1
17.	D	1
18.	D	1
19.	C	1
20.	B	1
21.	A	1
22.	C	1
23.	C	1
24.	D	1
25.	C	1

Section 2

Question			Expected answer(s)	Max mark	Additional guidance
1.	(a)	(i)	Statement relating to quartiles e.g. 25% lay more than/UQ is 200 eggs e.g. 50% lay more than 170 eggs OR Median value is 170 eggs (laid) e.g. 75% lay more than/LQ is 125 eggs e.g. 50% lay between 125 and 200 OR Equivalents 'in opposite direction' OR Range of eggs (laid) is between 20 and 240/range of eggs (laid) is 220 OR Minimum and maximum values are 20 and 240 eggs (laid) OR No. of eggs (laid) is very variable (Any two)	2	• If no reference to 'eggs' deduct one mark only Not: • average = median • 'average median'
		(ii)	Mean number of eggs laid/it is higher (than the median) OR Mean is greater than 90	1	

Question			Expected answer(s)	Max mark	Additional guidance
		(iii)	(Infection) reduces (fecundity)	1	Fecundity = no. of eggs laid
	(b)	(i)	Error bars do not overlap	1	
		(ii)	Increases (chance of)/more time for transmission (of parasite) OR More time for (parasite) reproduction	1	Transmission = spread/passed on to host **Not:** • allows transmission • reference to humans **Ignore:** • reference to intermediate/ definitive host
	(c)	(i)	Negative correlation between survival and the number of eggs laid OR Mosquitoes that lay smaller numbers of eggs live longer (1) Relationship is more negatively correlated in uninfected mosquitoes OR As fecundity increases the decrease in longevity is greater in uninfected mosquitoes (1)	2	Accept converse. Accept converse. Accept converse.
		(ii)	not reliable because many points lie far from the line OR reliable because a large sample was used	1	
2.	(a)		(Serum) provides <u>growth factor(s)</u>	1	**Negates:** • nutrients
	(b)	(i)	110,000	1	
		(ii)	Dead cells are not distinguished from live cells (unless stained) OR Small cells difficult to locate OR Numbers obtained are only an estimate OR Time-consuming OR Clumping of cells (Any one)	1	

ANSWERS FOR ADVANCED HIGHER BIOLOGY

Question			Expected answer(s)	Max mark	Additional guidance
	(c)		(Thin sections of) tissue OR Whole/unicellular organism OR Parts of organism (Any one)	1	Not: • named example of organism • named examples of parts of organisms
	(d)		**Replacement** (with another biological system, eg cell culture) OR **Reduction** (in no. used) OR **Refinement** (re techniques) (Any one)	1	Any description/example should relate to one of the concepts.
3.	(a)		Level/quantity of interferon (beta-1b)	1	interferon beta-1b = drug
	(b)		Allows (overall) effect of drug on (whole) organism/body to be observed OR Allows (possible) side effects to be seen OR Shows effects on non-target cells OR Nerve cells difficult to grow *in vitro* (Any one)	1	Not: • Reference to ecological validity
	(c)		Provides results in the absence of the drug OR Gives baseline against which effect of drug can be measured/compared OR Allows comparison between drug and absence of drug OR Shows drug was responsible for effect OR Allows measurement of psychological effect (of treatment) (Any one)	1	Not: • Presence of drug = treatment

Question			Expected answer(s)	Max mark	Additional guidance
	(d)		Patients may not (remember to) take drug OR Patients may not inject/administer drug correctly/effeactively OR May be different numbers in the three groups OR Some patients pulled out (before completing trial) OR Not all patients were (MRI) scanned/no scan data for 0·05 mg OR Patient self-assessment (is subjective/may be recorded incorrectly) OR Small sample size (Any one)	1	
	(e)		Informed consent OR Permission from patient to use results/data OR Right to withdraw OR Confidentiality OR Justification of research OR (Consider possible) risk/harm/side effects to patient (Any one)	1	
	(f)		Drug prevents/reduces **worsening** of MS/symptoms OR Higher levels of drug more effective OR Drug reduces **new** nerve damage (Any two)	2	Interferon beta-1b = drug **Not only** reference to single data point for conclusions based on Table 1. FOR Table 2: **Accept** reference to single data point but **NOT** dose related trend.

ANSWERS FOR ADVANCED HIGHER BIOLOGY

Question			Expected answer(s)	Max mark	Additional guidance
4.	(a)		Hydrophobic/Non-polar	1	
	(b)		Alpha-helix Turn	1	
	(c)		Binding (to one subunit of one oxygen) makes the binding of other oxygen more likely	1	Correct reference to affinity change for binding/release of oxygen. **Not:** • binding to other Hbs
	(d)		At low pressures (below 15–20) there is no difference OR Comparison of (maximum) O_2 saturation at 90/100 pressure units (95 vs 50%) (1) At high pressures (15–20 upwards) increase for normal is greater than for sickle cell (1)	2	
	(e)		Valine has no charge (on R group) so (haemoglobin) molecules don't repel (one another) OR Hydrophobic interactions occur between (R groups of) valines (causing clumping) OR Glutamic acid has a charge (on R group) so (haemoglobin) molecules repel (Any one)	1	Interaction between non polar R groups of valines is equivalent to hydrophobic interactions between valines.
5.			1. Cell division requires remodelling of cytoskeleton 2. Spindle fibres made of microtubules 3. Composed of tubulin 4. (Composed of) hollow/straight rods/cylinders/tubes **Maximum 2 marks from 1 to 4** 5. Attach to chromosomes/chromatids/centromeres/kinetochores 6. Radiate from centrosome/microtubule organising centre/MTOC 7. Spindle fibres contract/shorten 8. Separate chromatids/(homologous) chromosomes **Maximum 2 marks from 5 to 8**	4	**Pt 6** Radiate = extend = grow = originate = made **Allow** Radiate from centriole but **NOT** Grow from/made by centriole.

Question			Expected answer(s)	Max mark	Additional guidance
6.	(a)		Maintaining osmotic balance OR Generation of ion (concentration) gradient AND one from: • For glucose symport (in small intestine) • In kidney tubules • For maintenance of resting potential (in cells/neurons)	1	Not: • Maintain osmotic gradient
	(b)		Phosphorylation/conformational change (of pump) (1) **Lowers** affinity (for Na⁺ ions) (1)	2	Conformational change must relate to ATP binding/phosphorylation.
	(c)		Prevents binding of K⁺ ions (1) Preventing de-phosphorylation OR Prevents (reversal of) conformational change OR Affinity for Na⁺ ions (remains) low (1)	2	
7.	(a)	(i)	Aquaporin-(2)/AQP(2)	1	
		(ii)	Signal transduction	1	
	(b)	(i)	Urine output >3·5 litres (per day) on days without treatment/on day 1/2/5/6 OR Correct calculation of urine output per kg body mass on day 1/2/5/6 AND Stating value >0·05 litres/kg/day	1	Units required. e.g. from: day 1: 10·5/70 = ~0·15 day 2: 10/70 = 0·14 day 5: 8/70 = ~0·11 day 6: 9/70 = ~0·13
		(ii)	Urine production was <3·5 litres/<0·05 litres per kg on day 3/4 OR Urine production was <3·5 litres per day/<0·05 litres per kg per day during treatment OR Correct calculation showing urine output reduced to < critical level on day 3/4 (Any one)	1	'on day 3/4' **equivalent to** 'during treatment'
		(iii)	Failure to produce/lack of ADH	1	

ANSWERS FOR ADVANCED HIGHER BIOLOGY

Question			Expected answer(s)	Max mark	Additional guidance
8.	(a)		Gamete mother cell	1	
	(b)	(i)	Crossing over (at chiasmata) OR Breakage and rejoining of DNA/chromatids (at chiasmata) (1) (Leads to) exchange of DNA/alleles between (homologous) chromosomes OR New combinations of/recombination of alleles (of linked genes) (1)	2	
		(ii)	Independent assortment	1	
9.	(a)		(Much) greater proportion (of Mrcaru lizard's diet) is plant matter	1	
	(b)	(i)	(Mrcaru) lizards have micro-organisms to break down plant matter/greater bite force (1) These individuals AND are (better) **adapted** to new environment/eating plant matter/digesting plant matter OR have selective advantage/increased fitness (1)	2	suited ≠ adapted Accept description of *selective advantage*.
		(ii)	Short(er) generation time OR Warm(er) environment/climate/high(er) temperature OR High(er) selection pressure OR High(er) mutation rate OR Sexual reproduction/horizontal gene transfer (Any one)	1	
	(c)		Same mean as population as a whole OR Same degree of variation about/deviation from mean as the population (as a whole) (Any one)	1	
10.	(a)		Sexual dimorphism	1	
	(b)	(i)	Males gather/compete in (communal) area/lek (to display) AND Females assess/choose male OR To allow female choice	1	

Question			Expected answer(s)	Max mark	Additional guidance
		(ii)	(Display) increases **male's** chance of mating/passing on genes/reproducing OR (Display) increases **male's** breeding success	1	
		(iii)	(Surviving) offspring have increased fitness/more favourable characteristics OR High/greater number of surviving offspring	1	Characteristics = traits = genes = alleles
	(c)	(i)	(Sound) allows communication over (long) distance OR (Sound) overcomes difficulty of limited visibility OR (Sound) allows communication in spite of forest/trees limiting visual signals OR Allows female to locate male(s)/lek (Any one)	1	
		(ii)	(Dishonest as fake hoots) not indicating male mating success/fitness OR (Dishonest as fake hoots emitted when) females not present/no mating occurring	1	

11.	A	(i)	Costs/benefits of sexual reproduction:
			1. Males/50% are unable to produce offspring
			  OR
			  Only females/50% able to produce offspring
			  Only half of (each parent's) genome passed on (to offspring)
			2. Disrupts successful (parental) genomes
			  OR
			  (Combinations of) beneficial alleles/traits lost
			3. Increases (genetic) variation
			4. (Variation) allows evolution/adaptation (in response to changing environment)
			5. (Variation allows organism) to keep running in the Red Queen arms race (e.g. between parasite and host)
			Maximum 4 marks from 1 to 6
				9	Produce offspring = reproduce
					Genome = genes = alleles = DNA = genetic information
					
					Pt 2—NOT:
					• traits

ANSWERS FOR ADVANCED HIGHER BIOLOGY

Question			Expected answer(s)	Max mark	Additional guidance

		(ii)	Asexual reproduction as a successful reproductive strategy:
			a. Successful genome passed on
			b. In narrow stable niches
			c. When recolonizing disturbed habitats
			d. Vegetative cloning in plants
			   OR description of suitable example
			e. Parthenogenesis (in animals)
			   OR description of example
			f. (Parthenogenesis) where parasite burden is low/climate is cool/parasite diversity is low
			g. (In organisms using asexual reproduction) horizontal gene transfer allows exchange of genetic material/increased variation
			h. Example of horizontal gene transfer
			Maximum 5 marks from points a to h		

	B	(i)	Difficulties involved in treatment and control:
			1. Endoparasite defined as living within host
			2. Rapid antigen change/high antigenic variation
			3. Vaccines difficult to design/produce
			4. (Some) parasites difficult to culture (in vitro/laboratory)
			5. Similarity between host and parasite **metabolism**
			6. Difficult to find drugs only toxic to parasite
			7. Difficulty associated with vector control
			   OR
			   Indirect transmission
			8. Transmission rate high in tropical climate/overcrowded situations
			9. Overcrowding (can occur) in refugee camps/rapidly growing cities (in LEDCs)
			10. Difficult/expensive to improve sanitation
			Maximum 7 marks from 1 to 10
				9	Pt 8.
					Accept:
					• Spread more rapidly
					• Overcrowding = high population density

		(ii)	Benefits of improved parasite control to human populations: a. Reduction in child mortality b. Improvements in child development/intelligence c. Body uses more resources for growth/development **Maximum 2 marks from a to c**		

ADVANCED HIGHER BIOLOGY 2017

Section 1

Question	Answer	Max mark
1.	B	1
2.	C	1
3.	C	1
4.	D	1
5.	A	1
6.	C	1
7.	B	1
8.	D	1
9.	A	1
10.	A	1
11.	D	1
12.	B	1
13.	A	1

Question	Answer	Max mark
14.	C	1
15.	C	1
16.	B	1
17.	B	1
18.	C	1
19.	B	1
20.	C	1
21.	A	1
22.	B	1
23.	D	1
24.	A	1
25.	D	1

Section 2

Question			Expected answer(s)	Max mark	Additional guidance
1.	(a)		As extract concentration increases, the (percentage) increase in cells undergoing apoptosis increases	1	Ignore data
	(b)		Digest/break down proteins. OR Are proteases/proteinases. OR Caspases activate other caspases/DNAases/aspase cascade.	1	
	(c)	(i)	ci8 (+ extract) gives similar levels of apoptosis to extract alone OR ci8 (+ extract) has little/no effect on apoptosis (1) ci9 (+ extract) results in decrease in apoptosis (1)	2	Correct use of numbers acceptable e.g. ci 9 + extract results in 25% decrease
		(ii)	(Level undergoing apoptosis) is lower than in the untreated cells/control	1	
	(d)	(i)	350 (%)	1	

ANSWERS FOR ADVANCED HIGHER BIOLOGY

Question			Expected answer(s)	Max mark	Additional guidance
		(ii)	Cells with 400 units of DNA have replicated (but not divided). **OR** In 4A/treated cells 400 peak is higher than 200. **AND** Shows cells have replicated/not divided/arrested at G2. **OR** In 4B/untreated cells 200 peak is higher than 400. **AND** Shows cells have divided. (1) Peak/number of cells with DNA content of 400 units is greater in 4A/treated cells than in 4B/untreated cells. (1)	2	
2.	(a)	(i)	Opsin/photopsin (I, II or III)	1	
		(ii)	670 nm/it would be beyond the range of detection of all photoreceptors/green (and blue) cones (and rods).	1	**Accept:** • **Only** red cones detect light at this wavelength/670nm so no light detected. • Detected = absorbed perceived. **Not:** No light absorbed = v low absorption
	(b)		High (degree of) amplification.	1	**Accept:** Description of amplification pathway, e.g. (one photon stimulates/activates) hundreds/many G proteins which stimulate many enzymes
	(c)		UV/ultraviolet.	1	**Not:** numbers
3.	(a)	(i)	Cortisol/it diffuses through cell membrane. (1) Binds to receptor which switches transcription on/off. **OR** Binds to a transcription factor. (1)	2	**Accept:** Passes through = crosses = diffusion Alters gene expression = switches transcription on/off

Question			Expected answer(s)	Max mark	Additional guidance
		(ii)	(Different tissues will have) different responses **to receptor binding**. OR (Different tissues will have) different signal transduction pathways. OR Different genes switched off/on (in different tissues). OR There may be different cortisol receptors.	1	
	(b)		Does not have Addison's; Patient 2 cortisol increases by 75 µg per litre at 30 min and increases by 125 µg per litre at 60 min.	1	**Accept:** • Patient 2 increases by 75 µg per litre at 30 mins and a further 50 µg per litre at 60 mins. W.r.t between 30 and 60 mins • range of 125–130 range of 50–55. **Need:** Correct units (µg per litre) at least once.
4.	(a)	(i)	Kinase adds a phosphate to/phosphorylates (target protein; protein changes conformation).	1	
		(ii)	(Protein) phosphatase.	1	
		(iii)	So that sensitivity to the signal is restored. OR So that the (target) protein can respond again.	1	
	(b)	(i)	Charge/current (flowing through buffer) separates proteins (in gel) on the basis of size/mass/shape/charge.	1	
		(ii)	Antibody labelled (fluorescence/enzyme). (1) Fluorescence/colour/label detected if antibody has bound to PKA (showing its presence). (1)	2	**Accept:** Colour change = colour detected.
5.	(a)		Species may be elusive. OR Disturbance/harm/impact is minimised.	1	
	(b)		Systematic (sampling).	1	
	(c)	(i)	Long length of river sampled. OR 92/many sites sampled. OR Large sample size/number of repeats.	1	

Question			Expected answer(s)	Max mark	Additional guidance
		(ii)	Only 1 site showed latrines. OR No independent replicate.	1	
	(d)		• Latrines may have been washed away. • Some sites not surveyed due to deep water. • 5km between sample sites may miss vole territories. • No evidence that decrease due to predation/mink. OR No data for mink population. OR Other predators of vole may exist. (Any two)	2	
6.	(a)		Presence of (Sry) gene on the Y chromosome.	1	
	(b)		Temperature of (egg) incubation. OR Idea: ratio of males to females will alter at different temperatures.	1	
	(c)	(i)	Males lack homologous alleles on Y chromosome (so recessive allele always expressed). OR Males have one X so recessive allele always expressed. OR Males only need one (copy of) recessive allele (to be affected by the disease).	1	
		(ii)	X- (chromosome) inactivation is **random**. (1) Half the (kidney) cells will have a functional copy of the (ADH) receptor/gene. (1)	2	Accept: working = non-mutated = functional
		(iii)	50 (%)	1	
7.	(a)		Ethogram	1	
	(b)		(Use start times to) calculate duration of each behaviour to calculate proportion of time spent doing each behaviour.	1	
	(c)		Applying human activity/emotions/traits to humans so behaviour misinterpreted/conclusions not valid.	1	Accept: • human activity = perceptions = motivations = inferences
	(d)		Remote recording. OR Example such as • use cameras • use camera traps • video footage • satellite.	1	

Question			Expected answer(s)	Max mark	Additional guidance
8.			1. **Parasite** benefits at expense of **host**. 2. Example of parasite. 3. Parasite and host interact closely/frequently. **OR** Parasite and host **co-evolve**. 4. (In co-evolution) change in the traits of one species acts as a selection pressure on the other species. **OR** Idea of evolutionary arms race. 5. (RQ hypothesis states species must) adapt/evolve/change to survive/avoid extinction. 6. Hosts that are better able to resist/tolerate parasites/have greater fitness/survival/number of offspring. **OR** Parasites that are better able to feed/reproduce/find new hosts/have greater fitness/survival/number of offspring. 7. Sexual reproduction generates (genetic) variation. 8. (Variation) provides raw material for adaptation/evolution/natural selection. **(Any five)**	5	Pt 2: • To include bacteria/viruses/protists/platyhelminths/nematodes/fungi/arthropods • Named e.g.s acceptable • Flat/round worms acceptable.
9.	(a)		Trait disappears in group treated (with antibiotic then hypothesis is supported). (1) Compared to a control/no treatment/no antibiotic group (where no males produced). (1)	2	Note: • Trait = all female offspring. • Trait disappears = idea of males being produced again/sex ratio restored.
	(b)		Transfer of genetic material (from one bacterium to another) outwith reproduction/within same generation.	1	
	(c)		Purpose – to attract males (for breeding). (1) Females are competing so only occurs when males are in short supply. (1)	2	
	(d)		Protect/care for/carry young OR feed young OR build nest. **OR** (Greater) parental care.	1	Eggs = offspring = young. **NOT:** • Answers exemplified by *Acraea*. • Just parental investment.

ANSWERS FOR ADVANCED HIGHER BIOLOGY

Question			Expected answer(s)	Max mark	Additional guidance
10.	(a)		Epidemiology/epidemiological.	1	
	(b)		(Epidemics/outbreaks/measles) occurring (roughly) every 2 years.	1	**Accept:** Up one year and down the next
	(c)		As vaccination (uptake) increases, cases decrease.	1	
	(d)	(i)	Articles evaluated by experts **in the field**.	1	**Accept:** Academic = scientist = expert
		(ii)	With larger number of susceptible individuals. **OR** Number of immune individuals falls below the herd immunity threshold. **AND** Infection more easily transferred/spread/transmitted.	1	
		(iii)	(In Swansea) as vaccinations go down number of cases increases.	1	
	(e)		Herd immunity.	1	

11.	A	(i)	1. Tertiary structure is a folded polypeptide/3D shape.
			2. Shape/structure/conformation/folding determined by
			  One from:
			  • order of amino acids/R groups
			  • R-group interactions
			  • primary structure.
			3. **Two** R-groups named from:
			  • basic/positively charged
			  • acidic/negatively charged
			  • polar
			  • hydrophobic/non-polar.
			4. Named types of interactions.
			  One from:
			  • ionic bonds
			  • hydrogen bonds
			  • van der Waals interactions (London dispersion forces)
			  • disulphide bridges
			  • hydrophobic interactions.
			5. One other named from Pt 4.
			(Any three)
				9	Protein = polypeptide

Question			Expected answer(s)	Max mark	Additional guidance

		(ii)	a. Hydrophilic/polar (R) groups (mostly) at the surface of a soluble protein.
			b. (Soluble protein) found in the cytoplasm.
			c. (In soluble proteins) hydrophobic groups may cluster at the centre (of protein).
			d. Correct reference to membrane structure (with hydrophilic and hydrophobic regions).
			e. Membrane proteins are integral or peripheral (both terms needed).
			f. (Some integral proteins are) transmembrane + one example from:
			  • channels
			  • transporters
			  • receptors.
			g. W.r.t. integral proteins:
			idea of hydrophobic R groups interacting with hydrophobic region of membrane.
			OR
			Hydrophilic R groups interact with cytoplasm/extracellular environment.
			h. Peripheral proteins have fewer hydrophobic R groups interacting with the phospholipids.
			OR
			Peripheral proteins have hydrophilic R groups interacting with hydrophilic heads of phospholipids/membrane proteins.
			(Any six)
					Pt d.
					Accept labelled diagram
					Pt e.
					Intrinsic = integral
					Extrinsic = peripheral

	B	(i)	1. Membrane has hydrophilic and hydrophobic regions. 2. Polar/charged/hydrophilic substances can't cross/pass through (membrane). **OR** Hydrophobic/non polar substances can cross/pass through (membrane). 3. Oxygen/carbon dioxide/water pass through. 4. Protein channels/pumps/transporters needed for hydrophilic/polar/charged substances to cross. (Any two)	9	

Question			Expected answer(s)	Max mark	Additional guidance
		(ii)	a. Channels/pumps/transporters are transmembrane. b. Control ion concentrations OR Create/maintain concentration gradients. c. Different cell types/cell compartments have different channel/transporter proteins OR example. d. Movement through channels is passive/by diffusion/down a concentration gradient. e. Transporter proteins change conformation (to transport molecules across membrane). f. Conformational change in **active transport** requires energy from (hydrolysis of) ATP. g. Ligand-gated channels opened/closed **by binding of signal molecules/ligand.** h. Voltage-gated channels opened/closed **by changes in ion concentration.** i. **One from:** **Na/KATPase** • Maintains osmotic balance in animal cells • Generates ion gradient for glucose symport • Generates and maintains resting potentials in neurons • Generates ion gradient in kidney tubules. OR **Aquaporin 2/AQP2** • Transports water in the collecting duct. OR **GLUT4** Transports glucose in fat/muscle cells. j. Second example from i. (Any seven)	7	

ADVANCED HIGHER BIOLOGY 2018

Section 1

Question	Answer	Max mark
1.	A	1
2.	B	1
3.	D	1
4.	B	1
5.	D	1
6.	A	1
7.	D	1
8.	A	1
9.	B	1
10.	C	1
11.	B	1
12.	D	1
13.	B	1

Question	Answer	Max mark
14.	A	1
15.	B	1
16.	C	1
17.	C	1
18.	B	1
19.	C	1
20.	B	1
21.	D	1
22.	C	1
23.	C	1
24.	D	1
25.	A	1

Section 2

Question			Expected response	Max mark	Additional guidance
1.	(a)		All/most binding sites/GLUT transporters filled/occupied. OR Transporters (have specific binding sites for transported substance so) can be saturated.	1	Idea of binding to transporter being at its maximum. Accept: converse
	(b)		(Glucose) transport/uptake highest (in GLUT 3) at low (glucose) concentrations. OR Reaches V_{max} at the lowest concentration. OR (GLUT 3 has the lowest K_M so) it takes a small amount/lowest amount of substrate to reach saturating concentration/fill all the binding sites.	1	

ANSWERS FOR ADVANCED HIGHER BIOLOGY

Question			Expected response	Max mark	Additional guidance
	(c)	(i)	V at $K_M = 0\cdot02$ mmol/min so $V_{max} = 0\cdot04$ mmol/min $V = \dfrac{(0\cdot04 \times 5\cdot5)}{(17 + 5\cdot5)}$ $= 0\cdot0098 / 9\cdot8 \times 10^{-3}$ (mmol/min)	2	one mark can be awarded if: • incorrect V_{max} used • $V = 8\cdot31$ (17 has been doubled in place of 0·02) • $V = 4\cdot16$ (17 has been used in place of 0·04) • $V = 0\cdot0049$ (0·02 has been used in place of 0·04) Accept 0·01 Incorrect rounding = 1 mark penalty
		(ii)	Response/insulin production is only to high glucose concentrations (or converse). OR (High K_M ensures) glucose uptake high/increasing only at high glucose concentration.	1	
	(d)		(Insulin) **receptors** lose sensitivity (1) GLUT4 not recruited OR GLUT4 not transported to membrane (from intracellular stores). (1)	2	Lose sensitivity = loss of receptor function = do not respond Accept idea of: fewer
	(e)		As caffeine concentration increases the uptake of glucose decreases (then levels off).	1	concentration = Units as per axis label
	(f)		6 µmol (of caffeine) far too small to have an effect (on glucose uptake). OR No effect/not much effect as much higher concentrations are needed to give significant inhibition.	1	
2.	(a)	(i)	Cooperativity/cooperative binding	1	**NOT:** cooperation
		(ii)	(Acid/lower pH means) **Lower** affinity for/binding to oxygen in haemoglobin (so greater release of oxygen).	1	Haemoglobin = Hb/HB
		(iii)	Prosthetic group	1	
	(b)	(i)	Malaria	1	

Question			Expected response	Max mark	Additional guidance
		(ii)	(Drugs) reduce the formation/production of haemozoin OR (Toxic) haem builds up OR Prevents the conversion of the haem OR Inhibits HDP/production of HDP. (1) Haem kills the parasite. (1)	2	Reduce=Inhibit= prevent=slow haem = toxic product
3.	(a)	(i)	Resting (potential)	1	
		(ii)	100 mV	1	Units essential
		(iii)	(K^+ ion concentration is greater inside the cell than outside so K^+) ions flow **out** of the cell/in opposite direction (1) and return (membrane) to resting potential OR Restores membrane potential/polarity/repolarisation. (1)	2	NOT: reference to Na^+ ions
	(b)		Blocks/damages (voltage-gated) Na^+ channel OR prevents (voltage-gated) Na^+ channel opening.	1	NOT: reference to ligand-gated NOT: prevents nerve transmission alone
4.	(a)	(i)	Quaternary (structure)	1	
		(ii)	Hydrophobic/non-polar	1	
	(b)		Different (combinations of) exons are included/spliced together/in the mRNA. (1) Result in different sequences of amino acids/ R-groups OR Results in different folding/bonding/conformation/ structure. (1)	2	Coding regions = exons Amino acid sequence = primary structure R-group sequence = R-group interactions Conformation = shape
	(c)		(Binding) changes the conformation (of the receptor/protein).	1	Conformation = shape
	(d)		Positive modulator OR (Allosteric) activator OR agonist.	1	

ANSWERS FOR ADVANCED HIGHER BIOLOGY

Question			Expected response	Max mark	Additional guidance
5.	(a)		Tubulin	1	
	(b)		MTOC/microtubule organising centre/centrosome.	1	
	(c)	(i)	<u>Negative</u> control OR To show results without treatment/antibody (for comparison). OR To show the effect is due to the antibody/not due to the buffer.	1	Ignore reference to pH NOT just; as a comparison to cells with antibody
		(ii)	Cytoplasmic dynein plays a role (in spindle formation) in prophase/before metaphase/not in metaphase and anaphase. OR There may be a critical level of cytoplasmic dynein required (for mitosis to proceed).	1	
	(d)		Cytokinesis	1	
6.	(a)	(i)	Remission/cure brought about because of product/Vivafel.	1	**IGNORE:** mechanism of action
		(ii)	ANY ONE from: • no control/evidence of cat without treatment • no control of confounding variables.	1	**NOT:** no repeats/replicates **NOT:** only treats bone cancer Mention of amputation requires clarification as to impact.
	(b)		Cats will not have expectations/understanding of treatment/psychological effect not possible.	1	
	(c)	(i)	(Refinement) — harm minimized/reduced OR (Reduction) — minimum cat numbers for validity OR **owner** gives informed consent/can withdraw cat.	1	2R's need exemplifying **NOT** replacement
		(ii)	The treatment/Vivafel will have no effect on cancer (in the subjects).	1	Must refer to cancer

Question			Expected response	Max mark	Additional guidance
7.			**ANY TWO FROM:** 1. (Representative) sample should have same mean as population. 2. (Representative) sample should have same degree of variation about the mean as population. 3. Sample size bigger in more variable populations (to be reliable) **OR** Greater reliability with larger/more numerous samples. 4. Reliable sampling — similar/consistent values obtained. **MAX 2 MARKS** **AND** **ANY TWO FROM:** 5. Sampling: random/randomised — all individuals have equal chance of being selected/avoid selection bias. 6. Sampling: systematic/systematically — individuals selected at regular intervals. 7. Sampling: stratified — population divided into categories and sampled proportionately. 8. Naming of; Random, Systematic and Stratified sampling. **MAX 2 MARKS**	4	Pts. 4–6 If sampling strategies only described, penalise once for lack of name. Pt. 7 **only** awarded if none of pts 4–6 awarded.
8.	(a)		(Longer-necked animals obtain better feeding so) survival increased/selective advantage. (1) Improved fitness/more surviving offspring. (1)	2	Answer must be comparative for both marks to be awarded. Penalise once for no comparison.
	(b)		Increased competition for (reduced number of) trees. **OR** Increased selection pressure for long(er) necks.	1	
	(c)	(i)	Longer-necked (male) giraffes have better success in male-male rivalry, so get a mate/access to females/to reproduce.	1	

		(ii)	If NFS hypothesis were supported:
			  only males would have long necks
			OR
			  females would have shorter necks.
			OR
			If NFS hypothesis not supported:
			  females have long necks but do not use them for fighting.
				1	

ANSWERS FOR ADVANCED HIGHER BIOLOGY

Question			Expected response	Max mark	Additional guidance
9.	(a)		Males/half the population not able to produce offspring. (1) (Only) half of each parent's genome passed to offspring. OR Successful genomes disrupted. (1)	2	Accept: reproduce = able to produce offspring NOT: genes or traits
	(b)		Sexual reproduction increases variation. (1) To keep/maintain resistance to/tolerance of parasites OR To allow co-evolution between snail and parasite. (1)	2	Accept: description of co-evolution — must be in context of question
	(c)		Parasites (of these snails) absent/low density (in non-native habitats) OR (Parthenogenesis more common when) parasite density low.	1	
10.	(a)		<u>80</u>(nm)	1	Units not required (in stem)
	(b)		(The virus): Does not use /have reverse transcriptase. OR Does not use RNA (as a template) to produce DNA. OR Does not integrate DNA into host (DNA).	1	Accept: Converse argument. Accept: virus does not convert RNA into DNA
	(c)		(destruction of cell by) digestive enzymes/proteinases/proteases/caspases/DNAases.	1	
	(d)		Each new (viral) mutation would require a new vaccine OR vaccine antigens no longer match (virus) antigens OR once mutations occur, existing vaccines become ineffective OR vaccines might not contain all versions of the (target/viral) antigen/protein.	1	NOT: drug = vaccine

Question			Expected response	Max mark	Additional guidance
	(e)		AGREE or DISAGREE must be stated or clear from answer. AGREE: Trials with randomised control groups would be slower so more people would die (and this would be unethical). If treatment 'successful', control group would have higher death rate (and this would be unethical). DISAGREE: Evidence without a control group is weak/invalid. Safety/harm issues may only be revealed by presence of control group.	1	Idea of: individuals of control group will die
	(f)		Reduce overcrowding OR increase awareness of disease/education OR (measures to prevent transmission) protective clothing/quarantine/improved sanitation OR reduced contact with (infected) wildlife (eg bushmeat)/control infection in wildlife.	1	IGNORE: reference to vectors
11.	A	(i)	Realised and fundamental niche 1. Niche defined as the multi-dimensional summary of the tolerances and requirements of a species. 2. Fundamental niche is that occupied in the absence of interspecific competition. 3. Realised niche is that occupied in response to interspecific competition. 4. Where two realised niches are (very) similar competitive exclusion may occur/one species may become locally extinct. 5. Resource partitioning may allow species with sufficiently different realised niches to co-exist. Any 3	3	Pts 2. and 3. • NOT intraspecific (penalise only once) • The term interspecific must be used once. • Accept description of competition in context of resources used.

ANSWERS FOR ADVANCED HIGHER BIOLOGY

Question			Expected response	Max mark	Additional guidance
		(ii)	Features of parasite niches a. Parasites (are symbionts that) gain resources/nutrients at the expense of their host. b. (Often) narrow niche **and** host specificity. c. (So) parasites **can be** degenerate. d. Ectoparasites live on (the surface of) their host. e. Endoparasites live within their host. f. Definitive host — on/in which parasite reaches sexual maturity/produces gametes/undergoes sexual reproduction. g. Intermediate host — also required to complete parasite's lifecycle. h. Some parasites require/use a vector for transmission. **Any 6**	6	Pt a. • **NOT** just 'benefit' Pt c. • Accept: description of degenerate • **NOT**: degenerative Pt f. • definitive = primary Pt g. • Accept completing developmental stages of lifecycle • Intermediate = secondary • **NOT**: where asexual reproduction takes place

	B	(i)	The activity of homologous chromosomes
			
			1. (Homologous chromosomes) have the same size/centromere position/genes at same loci.
			2. Pairing of (homologous chromosomes).
			3. Chiasmata form where chromosomes/(non-sister) chromatids touch.
			4. Chromatids break and rejoin
			   OR
			   crossing over occurs.
			5. Exchange of DNA between (homologous) chromosomes/non-sister chromatids.
			6. (Leads to) new combinations of/recombination of alleles (of linked genes).
			7. (Homologous chromosome pairs) line up randomly on spindle/equator/metaphase plate.
			8. Independent assortment.
			9. **Separation** of parental chromosomes irrespective of maternal and paternal origin.
			
			Any 7
				7	Pt 1. Length = size
					Pt 2. Idea of active process
					
					Pt 5. **NOT**: Shuffling

		(ii)	Meiosis II a. Chromosomes line up **singly** on equator. b. (Sister) chromatids/chromosomes separate. c. (And are) randomly distributed to the daughter cells/gametes. d. (Four) haploid gametes formed. **Any 2**	2	Pt b. separate = pulled apart

Acknowledgements

Permission has been sought from all relevant copyright holders and Hodder Gibson is grateful for the use of the following:

Image © petarg/Shutterstock.com (2016 Section 2 page 12);

Two images © Bildagentur Zoonar GmbH/Shutterstock.com (2016 Section 2 page 22);

Image © Ian Schofield/Shutterstock.com (2017 Section 2 page 14);

Image © Stephan Morris/Shutterstock.com (2017 Section 2 page 14);

Image © Eric Isselee/Shutterstock.com (2017 Section 2 page 18);

A quote from 'Life Ascending – The Ten Great Inventions of Evolution' by Nick Lane, published by Profile Books Ltd © Nick Lane, 2009, 2010 (2017 Section 2 page 20);

Illustration reprinted by permission from Birkhäuser Verlag: Springer Nature 'Cellular and Molecular Life Sciences' 66: 1337 ('Ribbon representation of Cry3Aa toxin structure' fig. 1 by Soberón, M., Gill, S.S. & Bravo, A.) © Birkhäuser Verlag, Basel (2009) (2018 Section 1 page 3);

Image © Blamb/Shutterstock.com (2018 Section 2 page 6);

Image © azure1/Shutterstock.com (2018 Section 2 page 12);

Image © AndreAnita/Shutterstock.com (2018 Section 2 page 18);

Image © Roman Balla/Shutterstock.com (2018 Section 2 page 18);

Image © Designua/Shutterstock.com (2018 Section 2 page 22).